REUBEN A. KE

UNIVERSITY OF CHIC

THE CYCLICAL BEHAVIOR
OF THE
TERM STRUCTURE
OF INTEREST RATES

OCCASIONAL PAPER 91

NATIONAL BUREAU OF ECONOMIC RESEARCH

NEW YORK 1965

Distributed by COLUMBIA UNIVERSITY PRESS

LONDON AND NEW YORK

RELATION OF THE DIRECTORS TO THE WORK AND PUBLICATIONS OF THE NATIONAL BUREAU OF ECONOMIC RESEARCH

1. The object of the National Bureau of Economic Research is to ascertain and to present to the public important economic facts and their interpretation in a scientific and impartial manner. The Board of Directors is charged with the responsibility of ensuring that the work of the National Bureau is carried on in strict conformity with this object.

2. To this end the Board of Directors shall appoint one or more Directors of Research.

3. The Director or Directors of Research shall submit to the members of the Board, or to its Executive Committee, for their formal adoption, all specific proposals concerning researches to be instituted.

4. No report shall be published until the Director or Directors of Research shall have submitted to the Board a summary drawing attention to the character of the data and their utilization in the report, the nature and treatment of the problems involved, the main conclusions, and such other information as in their opinion would serve to determine the suitability of the report for publication in accordance with the principles of the National Bureau.

5. A copy of any manuscript proposed for publication shall also be submitted to each member of the Board. For each manuscript to be so submitted a special committee shall be appointed by the President, or at his designation by the Executive Director, consisting of three Directors selected as nearly as may be one from each general division of the Board. The names of the special manuscript committee shall be stated to each Director when the summary and report described in paragraph (4) are sent to him. It shall be the duty of each member of the committee to read the manuscript. If each member of the special committee signifies his approval within thirty days, the manuscript may be published. If each member of the special committee has not signified his approval within thirty days of the transmittal of the report and manuscript, the Director of Research shall then notify each member of the Board, requesting approval or disapproval of publication, and thirty additional days shall be granted for this purpose. The manuscript shall then not be published unless at least a majority of the entire Board and a two-thirds majority of those members of the Board who shall have voted on the proposal within the time fixed for the receipt of votes on the publication proposed shall have approved.

6. No manuscript may be published, though approved by each member of the special committee, until forty-five days have elapsed from the transmittal of the summary and report. The interval is allowed for the receipt of any memorandum of dissent or reservation, together with a brief statement of his reasons, that any member may wish to express; and such memorandum of dissent or reservation shall be published with the manuscript if he so desires. Publication does not, however, imply that each member of the Board has read the manuscript, or that either members of the Board in general, or of the special committee, have passed upon its validity in every detail.

7. A copy of this resolution shall, unless otherwise determined by the Board, be printed in each copy of every National Bureau book.

(Resolution adopted October 25, 1926,
as revised February 6, 1933, and February 24, 1941)

This report is one of a series emerging from an investigation of interest rates made possible by a grant to the National Bureau from the Life Insurance Association of America. The Association is not, however, responsible for any of the statements made or views expressed.

ACKNOWLEDGMENTS

THIS IS ONE of a series of studies in the behavior of interest rates in progress at the National Bureau of Economic Research under the administration of Joseph W. Conard and William H. Brown, Jr., of Swarthmore College. This research is being financed by a grant from the Life Insurance Association of America. Other studies in this series, and those responsible for them, include (1) an analysis of residential mortgage yields, Jack Guttentag of the University of Pennsylvania and Morris Beck of Rutgers University; (2) direct placement yields, Avery B. Cohan of the University of North Carolina; (3) the cyclical behavior of interest rates, Phillip Cagan of Brown University; (4) seasonal variations in interest rates, William Brown; (5) yield spreads between new and outstanding corporate bonds, Joseph Conard. A summary report on the interest rate series is being prepared by Conard.

Members of the advisory committee for these studies in the behavior of interest rates are W. Braddock Hickman, chairman, Federal Reserve Bank of Cleveland; Julian D. Anthony, Hartford Life Insurance Company; Daniel H. Brill, Board of Governors of the Federal Reserve System, Lester V. Chandler, Princeton University; W. A. Clarke, W. A. Clarke Mortgage Company; George T. Conklin, Jr., The Guardian Life Insurance Company of America; Milton Friedman, The University of Chicago; Raymond W. Goldsmith, National Bureau of Economic Research; Sidney Homer, Salomon Brothers & Hutzler; Norris Johnson, First National City Bank of New York; Robert G. Link, Federal Reserve Bank of New York; Roger F. Murray, National Bureau of Economic Research; James J. O'Leary, Life Insurance Association of America; Roy L. Reierson, Bankers Trust Company; Eli Shapiro, Harvard University; Henry C. Wallich, Yale University; and C. Richard Youngdahl, Aubrey G. Lanston & Co., Inc. The members of the advisory committee have

generously assisted in planning and reviewing the work of the staff
of the interest-rate project, but their concurrence with the views
expressed in this report is not to be assumed.

The members of the staff reading committee for this manuscript
were Gary Becker and Jacob Mincer, both of Columbia University
and the National Bureau of Economic Research, and Hyman Min-
sky of the University of California. All were very helpful.

Earlier versions of this paper were presented at the money work-
shop of the University of Chicago, faculty seminars at the Univer-
sities of Pennsylvania and California at Los Angeles, and the
Econometrica Society meetings in Pittsburgh in 1962. I have greatly
benefited from the comments of colleagues at both the National
Bureau and the University of Chicago.

David Meiselman of the Office of the Comptroller of the Cur-
rency, Paul Cootner of the Massachusetts Institute of Technology,
and John M. Culbertson of the University of Wisconsin provided
invaluable criticism in their roles as discussants at the Econometrica
Society meetings in 1962.

I wish to thank Messrs. Melvin G. de Chazeau, George B. Roberts, and Paul A. Samuelson of the National Bureau Board of Directors' reading committee.

Joan Tron edited the manuscript, and H. Irving Forman drew
the charts. I am grateful to Judy Tompkins for hand computing
and data collection, and to Richard Kilgore for machine computing.

A grant of electronic computer time to the National Bureau of
Economic Research by the International Business Machines Corpo-
ration was utilized for computing the regressions in this study.

REUBEN A. KESSEL

CONTENTS

TABLES

Tables

CHARTS

INTRODUCTION AND SUMMARY
OF PRINCIPAL FINDINGS

THE TERM STRUCTURE of interest rates, i.e., the relationship between yields or internal rates of return and maturities of default-free securities, has been analyzed by what can be regarded as three independent theories. One that has had widespread appeal for theoretical economists has been called the expectations theory. According to this theory, long-term rates are an average of expected short-term rates; the holder of a long-term security will earn, on average, just as much as the holder of a series of short-term securities over any specified time interval. To illustrate: if one bought a one-year security today and another when the first matures, the expected return would be equal to the return that would have been obtained if a two-year security had been bought initially.

Another widely accepted theory, not necessarily inconsistent with the expectations hypothesis, is liquidity preference. This theory of the term structure of interest rates, which often is treated as a modification of the expectations hypothesis, rests on the postulates that (1) the risks associated with holding long maturities are greater than those of holding short maturities, (2) the community prefers to avoid risk, and (3) there are positive costs to society of obtaining the services of speculators. It implies that the expected yield to be derived from holding a two-year security is greater than that of holding a one-year security, or series of one-year securities, for identical periods of time. The greater risks associated with long-term securities imply that, on average, they yield more. This view, which has been associated with the name of Keynes, may be found in Hicks where it is linked with the expectations theory. Hicks treats the term structure of interest rates as being jointly determined by liquidity preference and expectations. Meiselman, in his recent investigation, rejected the liquidity preference element of the Hicksian theory.

The third theory is based on the premise that the market for default-free securities is largely "segmented," i.e., that there is little or no switching among securities with different maturities by the large institutional buyers that dominate this market. To put the same point in somewhat different language, the cross elasticity of demand is low, possibly zero; securities of different maturities are poor substitutes for one another; what happens in the bill market has little or no relationship to what happens in the long-term bond market. This suggests that variations in inventories or stocks of securities by term to maturity produce variations in relative yields. Yields of short- and long-term securities need bear no necessary relationship to one another; yields of short maturities can either be greater or less than the yields of long maturities depending upon the inventories of each that are outstanding.

The first chapter of this study deals with the evidence relevant for examining the validity of these three hypotheses. The evidence bearing on the first two is quantitatively greater and can be interpreted more unambiguously than that for the market segmentation hypothesis. This chapter begins by explaining what the expectations hypothesis is. This is followed by an evaluation of the evidence developed by other investigators for and against this theory. Then the evidence produced as part of this investigation is presented. Finally, all of this data is evaluated insofar as it bears on all three theories.

In the second chapter market institutions are considered. An attempt is made to rationalize the existence of liquidity preference by examining the evidence on the costs of speculative services, assuming that the market prefers on balance to avoid risk.

The third chapter is a description of the behavior of interest rates for default-free securities over the cycle, particularly for the period since the end of World War II when data have been relatively plentiful. The business cycle is the unit for organizing, whenever possible, the data on yield variance, average yields, timing of peaks and troughs, and yield differentials as they are related to term to maturity.

The Hicksian theory of the term structure of interest rates is applied to the cyclical behavior of the term structure of rates in the fourth chapter. The first part represents a working out of the implications of the Hicksian theory. The latter part is expository; it illustrates the implications of the Hicksian theory for the term structure of interest rates at business peaks and troughs.

The principal finding of this investigation is that a combination of two hypotheses—liquidity preference and expectations—must be employed to interpret the term structure of interest rates. Taken by itself, the expectations hypothesis implies that forward rates are the spot rates expected by the market. Yet available evidence indicates that forward rates are high estimates of future spot rates. Hence it is difficult to interpret forward rates as expected rates. Similarly, liquidity preference alone implies that short rates ought always to be below long rates; this implication is contradicted by short rates above long rates, i.e., by the so-called "humped" yield curve. By interpreting forward rates as the sum of expected rates plus liquidity premiums, that is, by using both hypotheses, the rates expected by the market can be detected. Moreover, this more complex hypothesis explains both the bias in the estimates of a pure expectations hypothesis and short rates that are higher than long rates.

Correlations between forward and spot rates suggest that the market does have some power to foresee, up to a year in the future, spot rates from a month to a year to maturity. This same conclusion is reached if forward rates, adjusted for liquidity premiums, are used to predict subsequently observed spot rates, and if the mean square error is computed. Using either criterion, expectations seems to predict better than an inertia model.

The behavior of interest rates in the United States over the last century indicates that, relative to long-term rates, short-term rates are typically high about cyclical peaks and low at troughs; that is, they rise relatively during expansions and fall during contractions. Hence, the common belief that the shorter the term to maturity, the greater the cyclical variability in yields is, in general, correct.

Data reflecting the prices of government securities during the last forty years, and high-grade corporate securities during roughly the same period, show that short maturities typically yield less than long maturities. On the average, yield curves have been positively sloped. Nevertheless, yield curves with negative slopes were not uncommon during the period from 1900 to 1930.

These observations of the cyclical behavior of the term structure of rates can be rationalized, assuming the market has some modest ability to predict the course of short-term rates over the cycle. High short-term relative to long-term rates—a characteristic of cyclical peaks—indicates that the market regards current short-term rates as abnormally high, and expects them to be lower in the future. Humped or declining yield curves imply that the market expects short-term rates to fall sharply. Low short-term relative to long-term rates—a characteristic of cyclical troughs—indicates that the market regards current short-term rates as abnormally low and expects them to be higher in the future. For at least the latest nine cycles, or since 1921, short-term rates for governments have been, on average over the full cycle, lower than long-term rates; this is a manifestation of the less than perfect substitutability of long- for short-term securities in the market. It can be explained by liquidity preference and the costs of providing the speculative services required to "convert" longs into shorts.

1

EXPLANATIONS
OF THE TERM STRUCTURE
OF INTEREST RATES

It is the thesis of this investigation that the term structure of interest rates can be explained better by a combination of the expectations and liquidity preference hypotheses than by either hypothesis alone. Alternatively, these two hypotheses can be viewed as complementary explanations of the same phenomenon—the term structure of interest rates. The evidence to be examined in support of this view falls into two classes. One is the findings of previous investigators; the works of Macaulay, Culbertson, Meiselman, Walker, and Hickman contain evidence relevant for evaluating the substantive merits of this thesis. The other class consists of evidence gathered as part of the present investigation.

A. What Is the Expectations Hypothesis

The expectations hypothesis has been enunciated by Fisher, Keynes, Hicks, Lutz, and others.[1] It has had widespread appeal for theoretical economists primarily as a result of its consistency with the way similar phenomena in other markets, particularly futures markets, are explained. In contrast, this hypothesis has been widely rejected by empirically minded economists and practical men of affairs. It was rejected by economists because investigators have been unable to produce evidence of a relationship between the term structure of interest rates and expectations of future short-term rates. (Others

1 See Friedrich A. Lutz, "The Structure of Interest Rates," in the American Economic Association, *Readings in the Theory of Income Distribution*, Philadelphia, 1946, p. 499; and Joseph W. Conard, *An Introduction to the Theory of Interest*, University of California Press, 1959, Part III.

have found it difficult to accept the view that long- and short-term securities are perfect substitutes for one another in the market.) Meiselman contends that previous investigators have not devised operational implications of the expectations hypothesis. Moreover, he contends, they have examined propositions which were mistakenly attributed to the expectations hypothesis, and when these propositions were found to be false, they rejected the expectations hypothesis.[2]

Briefly, the expectations hypothesis asserts that a long-term rate constitutes an average (a weighted average in the case of coupon-bearing securities) of expected future short-term rates. It says that forward rates (or marginal rates of interest) constitute unbiased estimates of future spot rates.[3] It is based on the assumption that short- and long-term securities, default risks aside, can be usefully viewed as identical in all respects except maturity. It implies that the expected value of the returns derived from holding long- and short-term securities for identical time periods are the same.

The word *future* should be emphasized in discussing the expectations hypothesis, since it concerns the effects of expectations about future short-term rates upon the current term structure of interest rates. To illustrate with a simplified example: assume that two-year securities yield 3 per cent and one-year securities 2 per cent. The forward rate on one-year money one year hence, or the marginal cost of extending a one-year term to maturity for an additional year, is 4 per cent; this is arithmetic, not the expectations hypothesis. The expectations hypothesis, as interpreted by Lutz and Meiselman, but not by Hicks, states that the forward rates are unbiased estimates of future short-term rates. For the preceding example, it implies that the market expects the rate on one-year securities one year hence to be 4 per cent. Four per cent is not only the forward rate—it is the expected one-year rate one year hence; i.e., it is what the market thinks the one-year rate will be one year hence.

[2] David Meiselman, *The Term Structure of Interest Rates,* Englewood Cliffs, New Jersey, 1962, pp. 10 and 12.

[3] A spot rate is a rate on funds for immediate delivery; it is today's rate for money to be delivered today for a specified period of time. In contrast, a forward rate is today's rate for money to be delivered in the future for a specified period of time. This time period could be anything, a day, a year, or a decade.

Conversely, assume a 2 per cent rate on two-year maturities and a 3 per cent rate on one-year maturities. Then the yield on one-year securities one year hence which will equalize the net yield from holding two one-year securities successively with that of holding one two-year security is 1 per cent. This must follow if one accepts the view that securities are alike in all respects except term to maturity.[4]

B. Existing Evidence

1. MACAULAY

Macaulay was among the first to produce empirical evidence that related long-term rates to expectations of future short-term rates. Before the founding of the Federal Reserve System, there existed a pronounced and well-known seasonal in the call money rate. The widespread knowledge of the existence of this seasonal implied that time money rates, which are loans from one to six months that are otherwise similar to call money loans, should turn up before the seasonal rise in call money rates. Macaulay found that time money rates did in fact anticipate the seasonal rise in call money rates and concluded that this constituted ". . . evidence of definite and relatively successful forecasting." [5] Macaulay was unable to uncover additional evidence of successful forecasting. He warned against concluding that forecasting was not attempted. Macaulay's contention was that evidence of successful forecasting is rare because successful forecasting is also rare.[6]

2. HICKMAN

W. Braddock Hickman, in a preliminary, unpublished, but nevertheless widely cited and read, NBER manuscript prepared in 1942, reports the results of his tests of the expectations hypothesis.[7] Like Macaulay, he sought evidence of successful forecasting; unlike Macaulay, he failed to find it. He compared observed or actual yield curves with those predicted one year or more ahead by the

4 These calculations ignore compounding of interest and intermediate payments in the form of coupons.

5 Frederick R. Macaulay, *Movements of Interest Rates,* p. 36. The reappearance of a seasonal in the money market in recent years has made it possible to reproduce Macaulay's experiment with a new body of data.

6 *Ibid.,* p. 33.

7 W. Braddock Hickman, "The Term Structure of Interest Rates: An Exploratory Analysis," National Bureau of Economic Research, 1942, mimeographed.

Explanations of the

term structure of interest rates, as interpreted by the Lutz-Mieselman variant of the expectations hypothesis. For such a comparison, expected yield curves must be determined at one point and actual yield curves at a later point of time. If the expectations hypothesis is valid, Hickman reasoned, then expected yield curves will be correlated with observed yield curves.

Hickman found that simply assuming that this year's yield curve will be the same as next year's gave what he regarded as better predictions of subsequently observed yield curves than the expectations hypothesis. This was one of the early uses of an inertia hypothesis as a benchmark for evaluating the predictive content of a substantive hypothesis. Hickman did not employ correlation analysis. If he did, as shall be shown, his conclusion that inertia is the better predictor would be more difficult if not impossible to sustain. In addition, he subjected the expectations hypothesis to two additional tests. (These tests, and the data employed are described in Appendix A.) All of his tests are based on the view that the validity of the expectations hypothesis hinges upon accurate forecasts. Meiselman does not regard this finding as relevant. "Anticipations may not be realized yet still determine the structure of rates in the manner asserted by the theory." [8]

3. CULBERTSON

Culbertson's empirical research is similar to Hickman's; both ran tests based on the assumption that forward rates are accurate predictions of future spot rates. Culbertson examined the yields of short- and long-term governments for identical periods of time. He argued that if the expectations hypothesis is valid, then yields to investors ought to be the same whether short- or long-term securities are held. (His calculations take into account both income streams and capital gains and losses.) He found marked differences in returns for the same holding periods. Since he found it difficult

[8] Meiselman, *Term Structure of Interest Rates,* p. 12. Hickman also had some doubts about the relevance of his test or any other test. The difficulties in conceiving of a means for testing the expectations hypothesis led Conard to contend erroneously, as Meiselman's work demonstrates, that only by assuming the market predicts accurately is it possible ". . . to build a theory whose predictions can be meaningfully tested." See Conard, *Theory of Interest,* p. 290.

to believe that speculators would operate in the government securities markets and predict as badly as his results suggested, he rejected the expectations hypothesis.[9]

4. WALKER

Walker's test of the expectations hypothesis also was based on the assumption that the market could predict accurately. However, it was more like Macaulay's work in this respect than that of Hickman and Culbertson. Both he and Macaulay revealed the consistency between the implications of accurate expectations and the expectations hypothesis; both observed instances in which the expectations of the market could be presumed to be accurate; and both found the behavior of the market was consistent with the expectations hypothesis.[10]

Walker's work deals with governmental interest rate policy during World War II. Around the beginning of that war, the Federal Reserve System and the Treasury embarked upon a policy of stabilizing, through open market operations and the maturity composition of new issues, the existing levels of rates on government securities. At that time, the yield curve was sharply rising; the bill rate was three-eighths of 1 per cent, one-year securities yielded 1 per cent, and long-term securities 2.5 per cent. If the expectations hypothesis is correct, the prestabilization term structure implied that future short-term rates were expected to be higher than existing short-term rates. In contrast, the stabilization policy implied that future short-term rates would be the same as current short-term rates. When the financial community became convinced that the monetary authorities could and would make this policy effective, it also became convinced that existing long-term rates were inconsistent with revised expectations of future short-term rates:

[9] ". . . the explanation of broad movements in the term structure of rates must be sought principally in factors other than behavior governed by interest rate expectations." See John M. Culbertson, "The Term Structure of Interest Rates," *Quarterly Journal of Economics*, November 1957, p. 502.

Meiselman, *Term Structure of Interest Rates*, p. 12, regards this and Hickman's work as tests of nonexistent implications of the expectations hypothesis.

[10] Charls E. Walker, "Federal Reserve Policy and the Structure of Interest Rates on Government Securities," *Quarterly Journal of Economics*, February 1954, p. 19.

long-term rates were too high. Hence, there was a tremendous shift
out of short- and into long-term securities by the holders of governmental obligations. Such a shift is implied by the expectations hypothesis, given the prewar term structure and its wartime stabilization.[11] This shift in large part converted the stabilized yield on bills
to a nominal rate similar to some other wartime prices.

Walker's results, unlike Macaulay's findings, cannot be interpreted as providing unambiguous support for the expectations hypothesis because they are also consistent with an implication of the
liquidity preference hypothesis. Liquidity preference as a theory
of the term structure of interest rates implies that the longer the
term to maturity of a security, the higher its yield. Yield differentials between long- and short-term securities constitute equalizing
differences that reflect differences in risks of capital losses. The
establishment of a ceiling on long-term bond yields implies a floor
or support price for their capital values. A price support program
for long-term bonds implies that much of the risk of capital loss is
eliminated. Therefore, long maturities become relatively more at-
tractive investment media.

Although Walker's results do not discriminate between expectations and liquidity preference, they do discriminate between expectations and liquidity preference on the one hand and market
segmentation on the other. If the holdings of governments by the
major institutions of the financial community changed as much as
Walker reports they did, this constitutes evidence against the
market segmentation hypothesis; if the market segmentation hypothesis is correct, Walker should not have observed a shift in the
maturity distribution of governments by the major institutions of
the financial community.[12]

---

[11] If a rising yield curve exists, long-term securities yield more than short-
term because the market anticipates offsetting losses on capital account attributable to holding long-term securities. The elimination of these anticipated capital losses implies that the yield of long-term securities is truly greater than that
of short-term securities.
Conversely a declining yield curve implies that future short-term rates will be
lower. Hence the holders of long-term securities trade a lower income on current
account for anticipated capital gains. The stabilization of such a yield curve
means that these anticipated capital gains cannot be realized, hence, that the
yield of short-term securities is truly greater than that of long-term securities.
[12] This interpretation of Walker's findings as well as the contention that his
results are consistent with liquidity preference does not appear in the original

The expectations hypothesis has been rejected for its unrealistic assumptions, particularly the assumption that short- and long-term securities of equivalent default risk can be treated as perfect substitutes. Many practitioners in financial markets, committing the fallacy of composition, reason that no one regards bills and long-term bonds as alternatives because they observe that many institutions specialize in a particular maturity spectrum. As long as some ranges of maturities are considered as alternatives by individual participants in this market, and in the aggregate these ranges cover the entire maturity spectrum, the market will act as though bills and bonds are alternatives. Yet every participant in this market may deal in a highly circumscribed maturity spectrum.

Mrs. Robinson has contended that the purchasers of a consol must know the course of future interest rates for ". . . every day from today till Kingdom Come." [13] Hickman and Luckett have enunciated, less colorfully, essentially the same argument.[14]

Presumably the size of the bonus a promising high school or college baseball player receives in exchange for his affiliation with a major league club is a function of his expected performance as a ball player. This interpretation, which is widely accepted, implies that the market predicts the performance of a ball player over his entire career. In order to properly calculate the size of these bonuses, the market must predict batting averages, fielding performance, and, in the case of pitchers, pitching effectiveness. Emotional stability, which appears to be irrelevant for determining future short-term rates, must also be predicted for ball players, since many become emotionally unstable in the face of severe competition and hence lose some of their economic value.[15]

---

paper. Walker regarded his evidence as supporting the Lutz variant of expectations. For another statement of what the market segmentation hypothesis is, see Conard, *Theory of Interest,* p. 304.

[13] See Joan Robinson, "The Rate of Interest," *Econometrica,* April 1951, p. 102.

[14] Dudley G. Luckett, "Professor Lutz and the Structure of Interest Rates," *Quarterly Journal of Economics,* February 1959, p. 131. Hawtrey also seems to be a member of the school that rejects the expectations hypothesis because of difficulties in predicting short-term rates. He argues that short- and long-term rates are determined in completely segregated and independent markets. See Ralph G. Hawtrey, "A Rejoinder," *The Manchester School,* October 1939, p. 156.

[15] The objection to the expectations hypothesis for the lack of "realism" in its assumptions has led to an attempt to find an alternative, more realistic set

5. MEISELMAN

Meiselman is the first investigator to employ an operational test of the expectations hypothesis that does not depend upon accurate foresight for its validity. If a relationship exists between expectations and the term structure of interest rates, then its existence can be detected despite inaccurate predictions. The understanding by economists of how expectations are formed and revised in the light of new information has improved enormously in recent years. Meiselman, by utilizing this knowledge, was able to make the expectations hypothesis operational even when the market could not anticipate future rates of interest correctly. He showed that expectations, whether or not they are correct, nevertheless affect the term structure of rates. His results constitute striking evidence that the expectations hypothesis has empirical validity.[16]

The expectations hypothesis implies that the term structure of interest rates constitutes at one moment of time a set of predictions of short-term rates at various moments of time in the future. For every instant of time, there exists a term structure or yield curve and a set of implicit forward rates. These forward rates are, if the hypothesis is correct, expected short-term rates. If two term structures separated temporally are compared, the earlier contains predictions of future short-term rates and the later the data, i.e., the realized or actual short-term rates necessary for an evaluation of the accuracy of these predictions. Recent work on expectations suggests that if a realized or actual short-term rate is above its predicted level, then the predictions for other rates, yet to be realized, will be revised upward. Conversely, if the actual rate is below the predicted, then other predicted rates will be revised downward during the time interval between observations.

---

of assumptions. See Burton G. Malkiel, "Expectations, Bond Prices, and the Term Structure of Interest Rates," *Quarterly Journal of Economics*, May 1962, No. 2, p. 197. The author claims his model is ". . . in closer conformity with the practices of bond investors who had always considered the Lutz theory chimerical." (See p. 218.) Conformity here should not be interpreted as predicting better; there is no test of the predictive powers of the models in the Malkiel paper. Conformity refers to the conformation of the assumptions of Malkiel's model with descriptions of how bond investors behave.

16 Meiselman, *Term Structure of Interest Rates*, Chapter 2.

To illustrate: Assume at T_0, say January 1, 1960, the following relationships between yield and term to maturity are revealed by the market:

Yields as a Function of Term to Maturity at T_0

1-year governments yield	1.0 per cent
2	2.0
3	3.0
4	4.0

The expectations hypothesis, given this data at T_0, implies that the market expects future one-year rates to be higher than the current one-year rate. Since the one-year rate is 1 per cent and the two-year rate 2 per cent, the forward rate on one-year money one year hence must be 3 per cent for the returns on these alternatives to be equal. Analogously, if the current two-year rate is 2 per cent and the three-year rate 3 per cent, then the forward rate on one-year money two years later must be high enough to compensate for the difference between 2 and 3 per cent for two years. Therefore, a one-year rate of 5 per cent is implied for two years hence.

Market Predictions at T_0 of Expected One-Year Rates

Expected one-year rate for	T_1,	the year beginning 1/1/61, is	3.0 per cent
	T_2	1/1/62,	5.0
	T_3	1/1/63,	7.0

Assume at T_1, a year later, that the following relationships between yield and term to maturity are revealed by the market:

Yields as a Function of Term to Maturity at T_1

1-year governments yield	2.0 per cent
2	3.3
3	4.0

Clearly the one-year rate observed in the market at T_1 (2 per cent) is less than it was expected to be a year ago (3 per cent). The difference between the anticipated one-year rate one year hence at T_0 and the realized one-year rate at T_1 (both rates are for an identical moment of time but are measured one year apart) is defined as the error. If recently acquired knowledge on the formation of expectations is correct, then forecasts of expected one-year rates for T_2 and

T_3, i.e., for January 1, 1962, and 1963, will have been revised downward during the year 1960, or between T_0 and T_1.

One can infer from the term structure of interest rates at T_0 and T_1 how much these estimates of future short-term rates have been revised.

Market Predictions at T_0 and T_1

Expected One-Year Rate for One Year, Beginning on	T_0	T_1	Change in Forecast, or Magnitude of Forecast Revision (per cent)
January 1, 1962 (T_2)	5.0	4.6	− 0.4
January 1, 1963 (T_3)	7.0	5.4	− 1.6

At T_1 the expected one-year rates beginning at T_2 and T_3 are 4.6 and 5.4 per cent respectively. The difference between 5.0 and 4.6 per cent measures the change in the forecast one-year rate for T_2; the difference between 7.0 and 5.4 measures the change in the forecast one-year rate for T_3. Hence, if the expectations hypothesis is correct, then errors and forecast changes should be positively correlated.[17] Meiselman found that his error terms (i.e., the difference between predicted and actual one-year rates) and his forecast revisions were in fact positively correlated.

The distinction between anticipated and unanticipated interest rate changes is crucial for an understanding of how Meiselman tested the expectations hypothesis. If forward rates a year apart are as depicted by Chart 1, then the expectations hypothesis would imply that there has been no change in the rates forecast. Yet the rates for one-, two-, and three-year maturities must have changed during this year; yield curves were not constant. Nevertheless the expected one-year rates for particular moments of time were unchanged. The observations that are correlated, i.e., the error term and the forecast revision, refer to interest rates for particular dates.[18]

[17] Meiselman defines the error as the spot minus the forward; the revision of the forecast is defined as the later forecast less the earlier.

[18] An implication of this distinction is the proposition that stock prices can vary over time with no change in expectations of future earnings, if the market expects earnings to fluctuate. Hence, insofar as investors anticipate cyclical changes in the profitability of enterprises, anticipated cyclical variations in stock prices should exist.

Meiselman correlated errors with contemporaneous revisions in forecasts. For the example used, there are two forecast revisions, – 0.4 and – 1.6, that are correlated with the error, – 1.0. The future spot rates whose estimates were revised will be observed in the market as spot, and not forward, rates one and two years after the spot rate in the error term can be observed. For the data Meiselman employed, the future spot rates whose estimates were revised will be observed in the market as spot rates one through eight years after the spot rate in his error term can be observed. In both the example and Meiselman's work, forward rates pertaining to subsequently observable one-year spot rates for particular moments of calendar time were observed a year apart. The difference between observations which pertain to the same spot rate are forecast re-

CHART 1

Marginal Rates of Interest with Stable Expectations

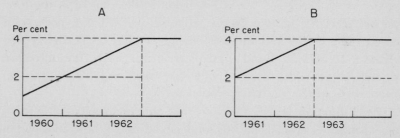

visions. Since Meiselman observed his forward and spot one-year rates yearly, he observed eight forward rate revisions and one error term every year (with, of course, the exception of the earliest year that his data encompasses). Meiselman produced eight regressions relating forward rate revisions to errors observed simultaneously. He found significant relationships for all eight, with correlation coefficients ranging from a low of .59 to a high of .95. All eight regression lines went through the origin, in the sense that the constant terms of the regressions were insignificantly different from zero.

This led to the inference that forward rates are unbiased estimates of future spot rates, which implies, when trends in interest rates are ignored, that yield curves are on the average flat. Short- and long-term rates will tend to be equal. If forward rates are biased upward, then yield curves, again ignoring trends, are on the average positively sloped. Hence, short-term rates will average less than long-term rates, and both, on the average, will rise with term to maturity. Such differentials between different terms to maturity, usually referred to as liquidity premiums, reflect the greater liquidity of short maturities.[19] Meiselman argues that the absence of a constant term in his regressions implies the absence of liquidity premiums. If the constant term is zero, a forward rate that is equal to the subsequently observed actual spot rate, i.e., a zero error term, implies no forecast revision. If forecasts are not revised when the error term is zero, then Meiselman infers that liquidity premiums are absent. To show that this inference is incorrect, consider the following formal statement of the hypothesis Meiselman tests:

$$_{t+m}E_t - {}_{t+m}E_{t-1} = \beta({}_tR_t - {}_tE_{t-1}) \tag{1}$$

Let E represent expected rates, R spot rates, F forward rates, and L liquidity premiums. The pre-subscript represents a year of calendar time. The post-subscript measures the moment a rate is either inferred from the term structure or observed as an actual spot rate. The forward and spot rates Meiselman considered were for one year only. Hence, $_{t+m}E_t$ is the expected one-year spot rate for the year $t + m$ that is inferred from the term structure of interest rates at moment t. The expected one-year spot rate for the year $t + m$ that is inferred from the term structure of interest rates at moment $t - 1$ is $_{t+m}E_{t-1}$. The difference between the post-subscripts t and $t - 1$ is, for Meiselman's study, one year.

One cannot observe expected rates directly; the term structure of interest rates reveals only forward rates. Whether or not $E = F$, or $E + L = F$ must be established by empirical evidence. Suppose liquidity premiums exist and they increase monotonically at a decreasing rate as a function of term to maturity. Then the longer the time interval between the moment a one-year forward rate is in-

---

[19] The Hicksian view of the term structure of interest rates implies that forward rates are biased and high estimates of future short-term rates. He viewed the "normal" yield curve as being positively sloped. See John R. Hicks, *Value and Capital*, London 1946, pp. 135–140. Lutz explicitly rejected the view that liquidity premiums exist because he could observe short-term rates above corresponding long-term rates and he regarded this as a contradiction of the liquidity preference hypothesis. See Lutz, in *Theory of Income Distribution*, p. 528.

ferred from a term structure and the moment it becomes a spot rate, the greater the liquidity premium. Similarly, year-to-year changes in forward rates for specific calendar years will increase as they get closer in time to becoming spot rates. The largest increase will occur during the year a forward rate becomes a spot rate.[20]

If the forward rate, F, is equal to the expected rate, E, plus a liquidity premium, L, then substituting in (1) yields

$$(_{t+m}F_t - _{t+m}L_t) - (_{t+m}F_{t-1} - _{t+m}L_{t-1}) = \beta[_tR_t - (_tF_{t-1} - _tL_{t-1})].$$

Let $-_{t+m}L_t + _{t+m}L_{t-1} = \Delta L$. Then the restatement of Meiselman's hypothesis becomes

$$_{t+m}F_t - _{t+ m}F_{t-1} = \beta(_tR_t - _tF_{t-1}) + \beta_t L_{t-1} - \Delta L.$$

Letting $a = \beta_t L_{t-1} - \Delta L$, results in

$$_{t+m}F_t - _{t+m}F_{t-1} = \beta(_tR_t - _tF_{t-1}) + a. \tag{2}$$

This is the regression equation Meiselman computed. He found that the observed constant was insignificantly different from zero. Hence, he inferred that a or $\beta_t L_{t-1} - \Delta L$ is also insignificantly different from zero.

A zero constant term is equally consistent with either $\beta_t L_{t-1} = \Delta L = 0$ or $\beta_t L_{t-1} = \Delta L > 0$. Hence, this piece of evidence is inappropriate for establishing the validity of the proposition that forward rates are unbiased estimates of expected spot rates; it is consistent with the existence of liquidity premiums. The proposition that forward rates are unbiased estimates of future spot rates remains untested.

Meiselman's own work, the work of Hickman, the time series of short- and long-term governments for the past forty years (to be presented in Chapter 3), and some new evidence presented here, all support the view that the term structure of interest rates, as interpreted by the expectations hypothesis, embodies biased and high estimates of future short-term rates. Meiselman used Durand's yield curves for high-grade corporates from 1900 through 1954 for his tests. For each of these years, Durand estimated a yield curve. If an

---

[20] For the purpose of determining whether or not forward rates are biased or unbiased estimates of spot rates, the liquidity content of spot rates is irrelevant. It is only the difference, if any, between the liquidity content of forward and spot rates that matters.

average is computed of the yields for each term to maturity, i.e., an average of all fifty-five one-year maturities, two-year maturities, etc., the composite yield curve which results, reflects average conditions for all fifty-five years. This curve is in fact positively sloped (see Chart 2). Since interest rates, if anything, were trending down

CHART 2
Average Yield as a Function of Term to Maturity,
Durand Data, 1900–1954

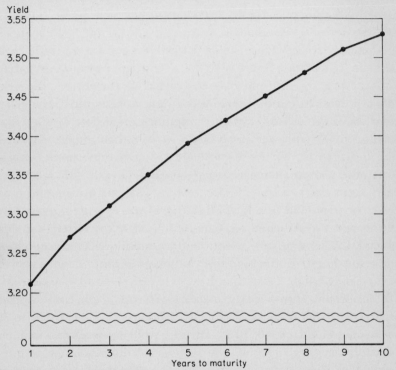

SOURCE: 1900–42, Durand, *Corporate Bonds;* 1943–47, Durand and Winn, *Basic Yields of Bonds;* 1948–51, *The Economic Almanac, 1956* (National Industrial Conference Board).

during these fifty-five years, forward rates must have been arithmetically high estimates of spot rates.

If liquidity premiums exist, the frequency of high estimates ought to be greater than that of low estimates and the average of the differences between estimated and actual rates ought to be positive.

Hence, Meiselman's error terms ought to have a significantly higher frequency of minus than plus signs and their average ought to be negative. Tests of these implications with the Wilcoxon two-sample and signed-rank tests lead to their acceptance.[21]

The foregoing demonstrates that forward one-year rates were on the average greater than actual one-year rates. It suggests that they were also greater than expected one-year rates and that they systematically overstate what the market expects one-year rates to be. This conclusion is based on an analysis of the inputs for Meiselman's independent variable. What about the dependent variable, i.e., the forward-rate changes that are regarded by Meiselman as prediction changes? Since forward rate changes are the difference between observations, separated by a year, of forward rates that pertain to a specific spot rate observable in the future, the first forward rate must be inferred from data further out on a yield curve than the second. Hence, if liquidity preference is operative (if it produces positively sloped yield curves), then the first forward rate ought to be, on the average, greater than the second. Meiselman observed prediction changes separated by one through eight years from the moment of time relevant for the measurement of the error term. The first forward rate is, on the average, larger than the second for all eight regressions. It is hard to rationalize this observation as a chance event; the probability of drawing eight successive negative numbers from a population in which negative and positive numbers are equally represented is less than 1 per cent. On the whole, this evidence is consistent with a positively sloped yield curve that flattens out as term to maturity increases; it is what one would expect to be derived from data summarized by Chart 2.

Meiselman's changes in forward rates and error terms constitute a measure of the marginal costs, more precisely the rate of change of yield with respect to term to maturity, of reducing term to maturity by a year. The pecuniary values at the margin, as revealed by the market, of liquidity changes attributable to changes in term

21 See W. Allen Wallis and Harry V. Roberts, *Statistics: A New Approach*, Glencoe, 1956, pp. 596–598. Significance levels of 6 and 2 per cent were produced using one tail of the normal distribution. Of the fifty-four forward one-year rates, thirty-five were high and nineteen were low.

to maturity of one year are computed. They behave, roughly speaking, as one would expect; the longer it takes for a forward rate to become a spot rate, the greater the premium of forward over spot. With but two exceptions out of a possible nine cases, liquidity premiums decrease monotonically as term to maturity increases (see Table 1).

TABLE 1

MEISELMAN'S ERROR TERM AND FORECAST REVISIONS[a]

	Years Until Second Observation Becomes a One-Year Spot Rate	Per Cent
Mean error term[b]	0	-.143
Mean forward rate revision[c]	1	. -.101
	2	-.078
	3	-.065
	4	-.077
	5	-.054
	6	-.040
	7	-.049
	8	-.022

[a]These data were obtained through personal communication with Meiselman.

[b]Mean of differences between one-year forward and spot rates.

[c]Mean change in one-year forward rates as term to maturity decreases by one year.

Hickman's data are consistent with Meiselman's findings. Predicted yield curves for the years 1936 through 1942, with a year between the time predicted and actual yield curves are observed, were all high. Even more interesting, and this is consistent with Meiselman's data, Hickman's results show that the longer the interval between predicted and observed or actual yield curves, the greater the bias in the estimates.[22] This empirical finding is an implication of a positively sloped yield curve when trends in rates are absent.

The data (to be presented in Chapter III) on yields of governments for the nine most recent business cycles, a period of roughly forty years, clearly indicate that the average yields of

[22] There are twenty-eight predictions, all too high. See Table A-1 which reproduces Hickman's data.

short-term governments are less than long-term governments. All nine cycles, without exception, conform to this generalization. These data constitute additional evidence that the term structure of rates, as interpreted by the expectations hypothesis, yields biased estimates of future short-term rates. If forward rates are not expected rates, but expected rates plus a liquidity premium, one should expect these time series to show that yields of short-term governments are usually less than long-term governments. Since Meiselman and Hickman worked with Durand's data, which reflect the yields of high-grade corporates, these data on the relative yields of short- and long-term governments for these nine cycles constitute independent evidence of the existence of bias in the predictions of the expectations hypothesis.

Unfortunately, this evidence is not unexceptionable. The fifty-five yearly observations of Durand, which Meiselman used, have a downward trend. In 1900, Durand's basic thirty-year rate was 3.30 per cent; in 1954, it was 3.00 per cent. If declining short-term rates are unanticipated, the predicted rates of the expectations hypothesis will exceed actual rates. From 1935 through 1942, the downward trend is still greater; the thirty-year basic rate fell from 3.50 to 2.65. Hence, if the long-term downward trend in rates has been unanticipated by the market, the relationship between the yields of short- and long-term governments may be a consequence of forecasting errors.[23]

Meiselman, like Walker, produced evidence relevant for evaluating the validity of the market segmentation hypothesis; unlike Walker, Meiselman points out the relevance of his work for this hypothesis. ". . . the systematic behavior of the yield curve would appear to contradict the widely held view that the market for debt claims is 'segmented' or 'compartmentalized' by maturity and that rates applicable to specific maturity segments can best be analyzed by rather traditional partial equilibrium supply and demand analysis where transactors act on the basis of preference for specific

[23] Hickman found that a simple projection of the previous year's yield curve produced numerically closer predictions than the expectations hypothesis, which is consistent with the foregoing interpretation. His finding is also, of course, consistent with an upward bias in the predictions of the expectations hypothesis.

maturities. . . ." [24] The correlation between forward rate revisions
and error terms demonstrates that changes in the yields of one- and
two-year securities are related to changes in yields of maturities up
to nine and ten years. Consequently, at least for this maturity
range, the market is not segmented enough to invalidate this test
of the expectations hypothesis.

C. New Evidence

Confining tests of the expectations hypothesis to circumstances for
which expectations can be presumed to be accurate has produced
only fragmentary evidence. Expectations can be presumed to be
accurate only under very special circumstances. Hence, forward
rates can equal expected spot rates and yet differ from realized spot
rates. But even this limited approach has not been fully exploited.
Clearly, in a world in which spot rates are positive, and this would
surely encompass the two most recent decades, one could assume
that the market never expects negative spot rates. Therefore, if
negative forward rates were observed, this would constitute evidence against the expectations hypothesis. Conversely, if negative
forward rates were not observed, this would be evidence for the
hypothesis.

The behavior of the term structure of bill yields during September 1960 contradicts the expectations hypothesis. In that month the
forward rate on one-week money, inferred from the term structure
of bill yields with maturities on December 8th and 15th, was often
negative.[25]

For nine of the twenty-one trading days in September 1960,
negative forward rates for one-week money could be observed. To
restate the foregoing, on these nine dates in September 1960 (and
this same phenomenon could be observed in September 1959) there
existed some bills whose asked prices were higher than the asked
prices for bills with one week less to maturity. Since it is unreasonable to argue that the market expected the spot rate for one-week

---

[24] Meiselman, *Term Structure of Interest Rates,* p. 34.

[25] The asked prices reported on the quote sheets of C. J. Devine were the
source of price data. Salomon Bros. and Hutzler quote sheets contained data that
led to the same conclusion.

bills on September 8th, or any other week since the end of World War II, to be negative, it follows that forward rates are not expected spot rates.

Critics have rejected the expectations hypothesis because the predictions of future short-term rates implied by the theory differed from subsequently observed actual rates. Meiselman argues that these critics have rejected the hypothesis for the wrong reasons. His position, that expectations need not be correct to determine the term structure of interest rates, is, of course, valid. Yet, given free entry and competition in securities markets, should not one expect to find a relationship between expectations as inferred from the term structure of interest rates and subsequently observed actual rates? It is of course unreasonable to expect expectations or predictions of future short-term rates to be absolutely accurate. New information coming to the market after a prediction is made will lead to prediction revisions and less than perfect forecasts. Yet new information should not lead to biases in the estimates; a mean bias should not be present. Hence, the average difference between predicted and actual rates ought to be insignificantly different from zero. The absence or presence of a mean bias in the relationship constitutes a test of whether or not forward rates are expected rates. Similarly, for very short intervals between the inference of predictions and the observation of actual short-term rates, there should be some observable advantage for the expectations hypothesis over some form of inertia hypothesis as a predictor of future short-rates. If not, why should the market waste its time and energy, which are scarce resources, in trying to predict future short-term rates? [26]

To control for trends in rates, and to measure forward and actual rates uninfluenced by capital gain considerations, the forward and actual yields of Treasury bills were examined from the beginning of 1959 through March 1962. All of the forward rates implicit in the

[26] Meiselman went too far in dismissing the work of Hickman and Culbertson. The expectations hypothesis, as he and Lutz interpreted it, does imply that there ought to be equality in the yields of short- and long-term rates in the absence of trends. If there is not, either the people operating in this market are doing an unbelievably bad job or this constitutes evidence against the Meiselman version of the expectations hypothesis.

TABLE 2

DISTRIBUTION OF ERRORS IN PREDICTING TREASURY BILL RATES[a]

	14-Day Rates	28-Day Rates	42-Day Rates	56-Day Rates	63-Day Rates	91-Day Rates
No. of observations	124	143	146	137	113	125
Frequency of high predictions	93	132	135	120	91	119
Average size of errors (per cent)	.199	.567	.599	.444	.455	.669
Average actual rates (per cent)	2.34	2.39	2.54	2.67	2.79	2.91

[a]Bills with precisely 182 and 91 days to maturity were used to compute the forward 91-day rate. Ninety-one days after this computation,
the spot 91-day rate was observed and compared with the forward rate.
Similarly, bills with 126, 112, 84, 63, 56, 42, 28, and 14 days to
maturity were used to compute forward rates and to measure spot rates.

Bid and asked prices, obtained from government bond dealers, were
averaged to obtain the prices used. The daily quote sheets of Salomon
Bros. & Hutzler, C. J. Devine & Co., were the sources of bid and asked
prices. These daily price reports quote bid and asked prices of bills
for specified days to maturity from the time payment is received.

Forward 91-day rates were computed by subtracting the current 91-day
rate from twice the current 182-day rate. This method of computing forward rates increases the difficulties of detecting an upward bias in the
estimates of the expectations hypothesis. It understates forward relative to spot rates. Indeed, if the estimates of the expectations hypothesis were unbiased, this computing procedure would show a downward
bias. Bill yields are bankers discount yields, and equal discount yields
for different maturities are not comparable. For example, a 4 per cent
discount yield on a 90-day bill implies a yield on a 360-day basis of
4.04 per cent. In contrast, a 4 per cent discount yield on a 180-day
bill implies a yield of 4.08 on a 360-day basis. In general, the longer
the term to maturity of a bill, the more its discount yield understates
its bond equivalent yield. Hence, the procedure followed produces lower
estimates of forward rates than would be produced by a correct computation.

term structure of interest rates during that time for two-, four-, six-,
eight-, nine-, and thirteen-week bill rates were computed and compared with actual yields. The time period under investigation began
and ended with the 91-day bill rate at the same level, approximately
2.75 per cent, although it rose sharply to 4.50 per cent and fell to
2.25 before it came back to its original level. The results of this investigation are tabulated in Table 2.

These results, along with the evidence already cited, strongly support the belief that forward rates are biased and high estimates of future short-term rates. Hence they are not the predictions of the market. In addition, these findings support the common belief that there exists a preference for short-term over long-term securities in the market. This preference produces a yield differential that constitutes an equalizing difference. The greater pecuniary yield of long-term securities represents compensation for the nonpecuniary advantages associated with holding short-term securities.

These findings also suggest that the futures market for money may be unlike other futures markets. Generally, one finds that forward prices are below corresponding spot prices when spot prices are rising and above them when spot prices are falling. For the futures market for money, however, forward rates in the Treasury bill market are typically above spot rates even when the latter are rising. During an upswing, the extent to which this occurs narrows, and some reversals, i.e., spot rates in excess of forward rates, occur. However, these reversals are suprisingly infrequent.

On theoretical grounds, one should expect liquidity premiums to vary with the level of interest rates. Treasury bills, like other securities, can be viewed as providing two streams of income: one is a pecuniary yield measured by interest rates; the other is a nonpecuniary yield as a money substitute. The average difference in 28- and 56-day bill yields can be viewed as an equalizing difference that reflects the greater value of the former as a money substitute. Economists customarily think of a rise in interest rates as implying an increase in the cost of holding money. By parity of reasoning, an increase in interest rates should also imply an increase in the cost of holding money substitutes. Since 28-day bills are better money substitutes than 56-day bills, a rise in interest rates implies that the opportunity costs of holding the former should rise relative to that of holding the latter. For this condition to be satisfied, yields of 56-day bills must rise relative to those of 28-day bills. Such a rise implies an increase in liquidity premiums, i.e., an increase in the spread between forward and actual 28-day rates. This reasoning is consistent with the results obtained for the range of bill maturities studied; the opportunity costs of holding any specified maturity, instead of a longer and hence less liquid maturity, increases as interest rates rise. Conversely, these opportunity costs decrease when rates fall. Within the range of bill maturities observed, and contrary to what is true for the yield curve as a whole, yield curves are steepest when rates are high and flattest when rates are low.

If the spread between 28- and 56-day bills increases with a rise in rates, and if liquidity premiums increase, then the premium of forward over spot money should also increase. This implies that what Meiselman and Hickman erroneously regarded as error terms, the difference between forward and subsequently observed spot rates, should be a positive function of the current level of spot rates. To determine whether or not this inference is correct, the difference between forward and subsequently observed 28-day spot rates was regressed on current 28-day spot rates. This is equivalent to regressing liquidity premiums plus or minus a forecasting error on current 28-day rates. These results are consistent with the hypothesis that liquidity premiums rise with the level of spot rates. The premium of forward over spot 28-day rates increases by one basis point for every increase of about five basis points in the spot rate.

The foregoing conclusion was derived from 137 monthly observations during the three business cycles from October 1949 through February 1961. They are supported by the results obtained from a regression using 138 weekly observations of 91- and 182-day bills from January 1959 through February 1961. For the latter test, the regression coefficient was about twice the former. A rise of about two and a half basis points in the 91-day bill rate is associated with a rise of about one basis point in the premium of forward over spot 91-day rates.[27]

[27] For the 91-day bills, the weekly observations cover a period when there were 182- and 91-day bills outstanding simultaneously. The regression coefficient was .43 with a standard error of .05.

For the 28-day bills, observations were obtained once a month. Typically, more than one observation could have been used in any month. The observation chosen was the one closest to the middle of the month. The regression coefficient was .22 with a standard error of .03.

The effects of bankers discount were eliminated from these data.

The association of a rise in liquidity premiums with a rise in the level of rates can also be shown by regressing the difference between forward and subsequently observed spot rates upon their sum.

The validity of these tests depends upon the absence of positive correlation between forecasting errors and spot rates. Unfortunately it is difficult to disentangle forecasting errors from liquidity premiums.

Since both interest rates and business conditions vary with the cycle, the finding that liquidity premiums rise with interest rates raises the question, are liquidity premiums a function of the level of interest rates or of the stage of the business cycle? In order to investigate this question, forward and actual 28-day bill rates were computed monthly from the term structure of 56- and 28-day bills for the three latest complete business cycles. During these three cycles, there was an upward trend in interest rates. Therefore, if liquidity premiums vary with the level of rates, it should be possible to observe that they rise secularly. The regression of the difference between predicted and actual 28-day rates on time for these three cycles does indicate an upward trend. Hence, liquidity premiums are positively related to the level of interest rates.[28]

The existence of liquidity premiums implies that the expectations hypothesis yields biased and high estimates of future short-term rates. It does not reveal in any direct way whether or not the market has any power to correctly anticipate subsequently observed spot rates. If liquidity premiums are held constant, if expected and not forward rates are observed, does a significant relationship exist between these expected rates and subsequently observed spot rates?

Forward rates for specific periods of calendar time and subsequently observed spot rates for the same periods were subjected to correlation analysis. This corrects, in a very crude way, for bias in the estimates of future spot rates attributable to liquidity premiums. Forward rates, which can be regarded as market predictions when adjusted for liquidity premiums, were inferred from the term structure of 182- and 91-day bill rates. (These rates were computed using an average of bid and asked prices adjusted for bankers discount.)

The results of this test indicate that the expectations hypothesis definitely does have predictive content. For 138 predictions of 91-day bill rates from the beginning of 1959 through the first quarter of 1962, the expectations hypothesis explained 58 per cent of the observed variation. The question remains whether an inertia hypothe-

---

[28] Of 137 predictions of the Lutz variant of the expectations hypothesis, 121 were high, five low, and eleven were correct. The effects of bankers discount were eliminated from these data.

sis could do equally well or better. Perhaps the observed correlation could be attributable to serial correlation in the data.

To determine whether or not the results obtained should be imputed to correct expectations, two variants of an "inertia hypothesis" were considered. One "predicted" 91-day bill rates 91 days hence by assuming no change. The other extrapolated into the future the difference between current 91-day rates and those 91 days ago.

The correlations for both variants of the inertia hypothesis tested were the same; each explained 48 per cent of the observed variation. The expectations hypothesis explained approximately 20 per cent more of the observed variation. During most of the period of observation, from about the middle of 1959 through the middle of 1960, there was a sharp rise and fall in rates. For the remainder of the period, interest rates were roughly stable. If the two hypotheses are compared for the period when rates were highly unstable (this reduces the number of observations to fifty), then expectations explain 48 per cent of the observed variations, whereas the variants of inertia each explain 30 per cent. The comparative advantage of the theory was stronger, as one would expect, when interest rates were unstable.

Is the observed difference between these correlation coefficients significant? Could it have occured as a result of chance? To answer this question, forward and current spot rates were correlated with subsequently observed spot rates and the partial correlation coefficients were computed. The addition of current spot rates increased the fraction of the observed variation explained from 58 to 59 per cent. The partial regression coefficient for expectations was significant and positive (the partial regression coefficient was .86, with a standard error of .14). In contrast, the partial regression coefficient for inertia was negative and also significant (the regression coefficient was − .31, with a standard error of .18).

These results indicate clearly that the expectations hypothesis does have predictive content that cannot be attributed to inertia. However, the negative coefficient for inertia requires explanation. The hypothesis presented here views the forward rate as a function of expected spot rates plus a liquidity premium. But liquidity premiums are a function of the level of spot rates: when current spot rates are high, the premium over spot that is reflected in the forward rate is also high, and vice versa. Hence, the larger the spot rate, the larger the number that ought to be deducted from forward rates to obtain the expected rates of the market. Therefore, the negative coefficient which is observed is consistent with the view that liquidity premiums exist and vary directly with the level of interest rates, more specifically with spot rates.

To restate this argument more formally, using symbols already defined:

1. $_{t+1}F_t = {}_{t+1}E_t + {}_tLP_t.$
2. $_tLP_t = f(_tR_t).$
3. $_{t+1}F_t - f(_tR_t) = {}_{t+1}E_t.$
4. $_{t+1}E_t = {}_{t+1}R_{t+1} + U.$
5. $_{t+1}F_t - f(_tR_t) = {}_{t+1}R_{t+1} + U.$

The data used to evaluate the predictive content of the expectations hypothesis are reproduced in Chart 3. The thick line depicts actual 91-day rates. The thin lines indicate forward rates adjusted and unadjusted for liquidity premiums. The point of origin of the thin lines at the thick line represents the moment a forward rate is inferred; the terminal point of the thin line measures the magnitude of the forward rate at the moment when the actual 91-day rate corresponding to this forward rate can be observed. Liquidity premiums were measured using the regression equation obtained by regressing the difference between forward and realized 91-day rates on current spot rates. These results suggest that within the range of maturities encompassed by Treasury bills, expectations do influence the term structure of interest rates, and the market forecasts future spot rates with some degree of accuracy. However, to obtain the expectations of the market, liquidity premiums must be deducted from forward rates.[29]

[29] The fact that forward rates are usually higher than actual spot rates may have led Hickman to abandon the search for a relationship between them. An inertia hypothesis could produce numerically closer predictions to spot rates than the expectations hypothesis, yet the latter could produce stronger correlations. It is the strength of the correlations, if one accepts the view that liquidity premiums exist, that is relevant for evaluating these alternatives. Insofar as liquidity premiums are a constant or linear function of forward rates, they do

CHART 3
Market Expectations of Future 91-Day Bill Rates

——————— Forward rates
———————— Forward rates adjusted for liquidity premiums
——————— Spot rates

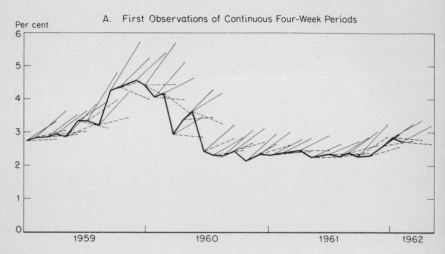

A. First Observations of Continuous Four-Week Periods

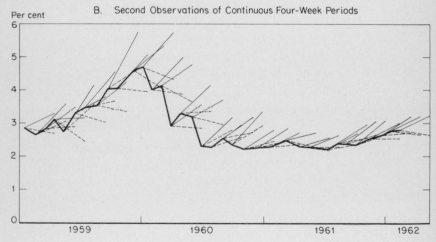

B. Second Observations of Continuous Four-Week Periods

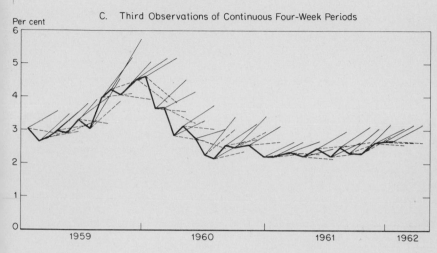

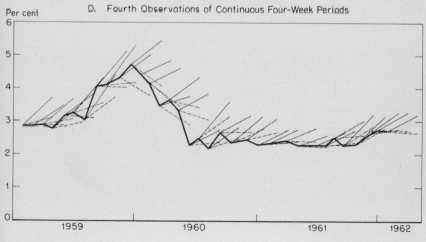

Thus far, this analysis does not reveal how stable the liquidity preference function is. Is the relationship between spot rates and liquidity premiums stable enough to permit one to estimate liquidity premiums for one business cycle and use these estimates to uncover successfully the expectations of the market, as distinguished from forward rates, for a second cycle? To answer this question, the regression of the difference between forward and subsequently observed 28-day spot rates upon current 28-day spot rates, for the two cycles from October 1949 through April 1958, was used to estimate liquidity premiums for the following cycle. Then inertia and expectations were compared as a means of forecasting subsequently observed spot rates. Expectations was definitely the better predictor. The standard error of estimate was .50 for inertia against .38 for expectations. The partial regression coefficient for inertia was −.07; for expectations, it was .75. The standard error of the regression coefficient was .19 for inertia and .16 for expectations. Multiple correlation analysis, using forward rates adjusted for liquidity premiums, yields results almost identical with those obtained with unadjusted forward rates.[30]

These results suggested that the data Meiselman employed, which were compiled by Durand, should be reexamined to see if forward rates do predict subsequently observed spot rates. Hence forward and current spot rates were considered as independent variables and subsequently observed spot rates as the dependent variable in a multiple regression equation. This involves using the same data Meiselman used to compute what he regards as an error term. No evidence of successful forecasting was detected; inertia appeared to be the better independent variable.

To utilize more recent data that are qualitatively more com-

---

not influence the correlation of forward with spot rates. For the two sets of seven pairs of observations in Hickman's study, representing one-year forecasts, the correlation coefficient for expectations was .725; for inertia, .721. When both variables were included in a multiple correlation, neither had a significant partial correlation coefficient. Hence no basis is provided by correlation analysis for arguing that one or the other variable explained the observed variation. If one plots forward rates and the variant of inertia Hickman employed, there is almost a constant difference between them.

30 For the three cycles, 1949 to 1961, the simple correlation coefficients indicated that expectations explained 88 per cent of the observed variation whereas inertia, i.e., extrapolating no change, explained 82 per cent.

parable to the data Meiselman utilized, the experiment performed
with forward and spot three-month Treasury bills was repeated
using monthly forward and spot one-year governments for 1958
through 1961. One- and two-year rates were read off the fixed maturity yield curve published monthly in the Treasury Bulletin.[31]
Again forward and current spot rates were treated as independent
variables and subsequently observed spot rates as the dependent
variable. The result is consistent with that using three- and six-
month bills and reinforces the view that the market has some power
to forecast successfully. However, taken by itself it does not constitute quite as convincing evidence of the existence of successful
forecasting. This is what one would expect; it is harder to forecast
a year into the future than it is to forecast for three months.

If the rationalization of the statistical findings using three- and
six-month bills is correct, then forward rates should have a positive
coefficient and current one-year rates a negative one. One should
also expect to find that the partial correlation coefficient for expectations would be smaller in the case of one- and two-year Treasury securities than it was for three- and six-month bills.

These anticipations are in general borne out. The sign of the regression coefficient for one-year spot rates is negative. For three-
and six-month bills, this regression coefficient is 75 per cent greater
than its standard error; for one- and two-year governments, it is a
third larger than its standard error. For three- and six-month bills,
the regression coefficient for forward rates is positive and six times
its standard error; in the case of one- and two-year governments, it
is positive but only nine-tenths its standard error.

Possibly the most convincing evidence that the market can forecast, with modest accuracy, one-year spot rates one year into the
future was obtained through the following experiment. Liquidity
premiums embodied in one-year forward rates for the 1958–61 cycle
were estimated from an equation derived from the difference between forward and subsequently observed spot rates regressed on
current one-year rates for the 1954–58 cycle. The expected rates of
the market for the 1958–61 cycle were then obtained by subtracting

31 I am indebted to H. Irving Forman of the National Bureau staff for these
measurements. They are reproduced, along with the related forward and spot
rates, in Appendix Table B-1.

the estimated liquidity premiums from forward rates. The mean square errors in the implicit forecasts of the market, i.e., the difference between forward rates less liquidity premiums and subsequently observed spot rates were compared with those generated by assuming next year's one-year spot rates will be identical with current rates. Although neither independent variable appeared in some absolute sense to yield very good forecasts, it is clear that expectations was significantly better as an independent variable than inertia. For thirty-five monthly observations, the mean square error was 2.09 for inertia, .91 for expectations. The elimination of liquidity premiums contributed importantly to this reduction in error. Without such adjustment, the mean square error of the forward rates was 1.91, only slightly less than that for inertia. These results show that if one is predicting one-year rates one year hence, and the current one-year rate is known, adding the two-year rate to one's knowledge constitutes a valuable piece of information.

Time series of forward and spot one-year rates during the period 1958 to 1961 are reproduced as Chart 4. These data, as well as the data for forward and spot three-month bills, suggest that the market can detect spot rates that are abnormally high or low. All of the forward rates are biased estimates. However, if one examines the slopes of the lines connecting current spot rates with forward rates for one year into the future, these lines appear flattest when current spot rates are highest. Hence, if the market can abstract from liquidity premiums (which produce the bias) then it appears that the market can forecast. That is, when rates are high, the market expects them to fall, and conversely, as the adjusted forward rates in the lower part of the chart suggest. This is consistent with the view that the market has some notion of what constitutes a normal rate of interest.

What causes the observed difference between the results using Durand's data on corporates and the recent data on one- and two-year governments? The evidence provides the basis for highly speculative answers at best. Durand's data encompass fifty-five years and are yearly observations; the data on governments encompass five years and are monthly observations. Possibly the market cannot distinguish between cyclically and secularly high and low rates

CHART 4
Forward and Spot One-Year Rates on Government Securities

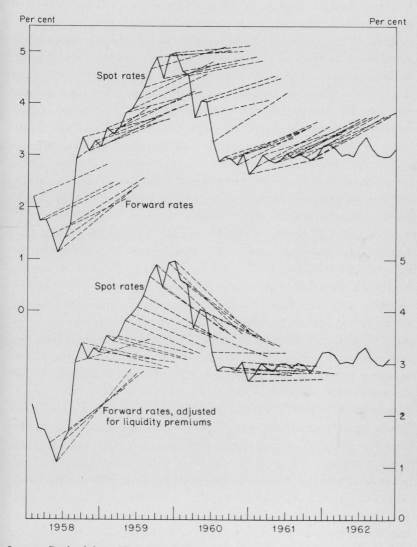

SOURCE: Derived from Treasury yield curves, using one- and two-year rates. The rates in the upper section of the chart are from Table B-1; those in the lower section, from Tables B-2 and B-3.

of interest. If the market could anticipate cyclical changes better than secular changes, there would be an observed difference in forecasting accuracy over one cycle as compared with many cycles. When spot rates are high cyclically, their subsequent change is quite different from that when they are high secularly. If the forecasts of the market are the same in either case, studies of the accuracy of forecasts will lead to different results depending upon the time period under investigation.

Another avenue for explaining secular and cyclical differences is the study of the stability of liquidity premiums over time. Before the 1930's, judging by Durand's data, liquidity premiums were much smaller or possibly nonexistent. There seems to have been a structural change in the economy in this respect since the early 1930's. Possibly this can be attributed to the abolition of interest on demand deposits, or perhaps to a change in attitude toward risk that led to changes in liquidity premiums. In any case, instability of liquidity premiums could account for the observed difference in the secular and cyclical correlations of forward and one-year spot rates.

Still another avenue for explaining these findings is data limitations. Durand did not use a criterion such as least squares for his curve fitting. He fitted only yield curves that do not have maximums or minimums. When his yield curves were not flat throughout, they either increased or decreased monotonically with term to maturity and then flattened out. By definition, Durand could not observe a yield curve with any other shape. He offers no explanation for this self-imposed constraint.

In the postwar period, when short-term rates have been above long-term rates, yield curves have been hump shaped. These curves at first rise with term to maturity, reach a maximum, and then fall and finally flatten out. It is difficult to believe that this was not also true during some of the fifty-five years encompassed by Durand's data. If one examines both the data and the curves fitted, it is clear that humped yield curves could just as correctly have been fitted some of the time. Since this was not done, one- and two-year rates derived from Durand's curves are probably high estimates of true one- and two-year rates, and are high relative to longer maturities.

If one examines the yield curves Durand fitted to data in the 1920's, yield curves for governments and corporates have opposite slopes for three of these years. Indeed, the data on governments presented above show short-term governments yielding, on average, less than long-term governments in the 1920's. Durand's findings on corporates indicate just the opposite.

Another difficulty, ignored by both Hickman and Meiselman, is the fact that Durand's yield curves are drawn for coupon bonds. Hence, the Hicksian formula for internal rates of return or yield to maturity, which implicitly assumes the absence of coupons, is inappropriate for computing forward rates. To compute forward rates correctly, both coupons and yields to maturity, or internal rates of return, must be known.

If one accepts the view that yield curves were, on average, positively sloped during the fifty-five years Durand observed, then coupon rates for bonds with one or two years to maturity must have, on average, exceeded internal rates of return. If coupons exceed internal rates of return, then it can be shown that the Hicksian formula underestimates forward rates. However, the measurement errors which can be attributed to ignoring coupons seem to be small compared to those attributable to uncertainties regarding the shape of Durand's yield curves. Using coupons of 6 per cent, errors in computing forward rates seem to be on the order of two or three basis points.

The figures on bill rates collected provide new data to repeat Meiselman's experiments. The results of tests of the expectations hypothesis using Treasury bills are tabulated in Table 3. Treasury bills with terms to maturity of less than six months are the source of price data.

Since these correlations are all unambiguously significant, they provide additional support for Meiselman's view that a relationship between expectations and the term structure of interest rates exists. His major conclusion—that there is validity in the expectations hypothesis—is sound, despite his failure to isolate unanticipated changes in interest rates and to recognize that forward rates were not expected rates. What about the data Meiselman used? How are the liquidity premiums related to the level of rates for Durand's

TABLE 3

CORRELATION OF FORECAST REVISIONS WITH ERRORS
AS DEFINED BY MEISELMAN,
1958-61[a]

Type of Error	Correlation Coefficient	Regression Coefficient
1. Error in forecast of two-week rates with changes in expected two-week rates two weeks hence	.37	.40
2. Error in forecast of two-week rates with changes in expected two-week rates eleven weeks hence	.36	.26
3. Error in forecast of four-week rates with changes in expected four-week rates twelve weeks hence	.21	.27
4. Error in forecast of six-week rates with changes in expected six-week rates eighteen weeks hence	.59	.62
5. Error in forecast of eight-week rates with changes in expected eight-week rates sixteen weeks hence	.85	.59

Source

Line 1: Correlation of changes in predicted two-week bill rates with
forecasting errors implied by the expectations hypothesis, i.e., with
the difference between predicted and actual two-week rates. The error
terms were obtained by comparing predictions implied by four- and two-
week bill rates with actual two-week bill rates two weeks later. The
prediction changes were obtained from the difference between the predicted two-week rate four weeks hence and then, two weeks later, two
weeks into the future. The first prediction was obtained through the
use of six- and four-week bills; the second was measured through the
use of four- and two-week bills.

Line 2: Correlation of changes in predicted two-week bill rates as inferred from eleven- and nine-week bills and, two weeks later, from
nine- and seven-week bills with the difference between predicted and
actual two-week rates. The independent variables for this and the test
described in Line 1 are identical.

Line 3: Correlation of changes in predicted four-week bill rates with the
prediction errors implied by the expectations hypothesis. The independent variable is the difference between predictions implied by eight- and
four-week bill rates and, four weeks later, actual four-week bill rates.
The dependent variable--the prediction change--is the difference between
the predicted four-week rate implied by the sixteen- and twelve-week bill
rates and, four weeks later, the predicted four-week rate implied by the
twelve- and eight-week bill rates.

Line 4: Correlation of changes in predicted six-week bill rates with prediction errors. The independent variable is the difference between predictions implied by twelve- and six-week bill rates and, six weeks later,
actual six-week bill rates. The dependent variable, the prediction
change, is the difference between the predicted six-week rate implied

NOTES TO TABLE 3 (concluded)

by the twenty-four- and eighteen-week rates and, six weeks later, the predicted six-week rate implied by the eighteen- and twelve-week bill rates.

Line 5: Correlation of changes in predicted eight-week bill rates with prediction errors. The independent variable is the difference between predictions implied by sixteen- and eight-week bill rates and, eight weeks later, actual eight-week bill rates. The dependent variable, the prediction change, is the difference between the predicted eight-week rate implied by the twenty-four- and sixteen-week rates and, eight weeks later, the predicted eight-week rate implied by the sixteen- and eight-week rates. This may be illustrated by the following sample calculation. On November 28, 1961, the sixteen-week rate was 2.61, and the eight-week rate 2.51. The expectations hypothesis implies that the eight-week rate eight weeks hence, on January 23, 1962, is expected to be 2.71. This is twice the sixteen-week rate less the eight-week rate. The actual eight-week rate on January 23, 1962, eight weeks after November 28, was 2.61. Hence the error is -.10. The first prediction in the data from which Line 5 was derived was inferred from the twenty-four- and sixteen-week rates on November 28, 1961. These were 2.72 and 2.61 respectively. Hence the predicted rate for March 20, 1962, which is three times the twenty-four-week rate less twice the sixteen-week rate, is 2.94. Eight weeks later, on January 23, 1962, the sixteen-week rate was 2.72, and the eight-week rate 2.61. Hence the predicted eight-week rate for March 20, 1962, was 2.83, and the prediction change -.11.

[a]The existence of liquidity premiums implies that the errors as defined by Meiselman are typically larger than the true errors the market committed. The true errors are the differences between forward rates minus liquidity premiums and spot rates; the true forecast revisions are the observed revisions net of liquidity differences.

data? The regression of the difference between forward and subsequently observed spot one-year rates against current one-year rates reveals little variation in the "error" with the level of spot rates. The regression coefficient is .09 with the standard error of .06, and only about 4 per cent of the variation is explained. In contrast, for the same regression using forward and spot one-year governments for the 1958–61 cycle, the regression coefficient is one, with a standard error of .10, and 70 per cent of the variation is explained. Clearly the different between forward and spot rates for the government data appears to be much more sensitive to variations in spot rates than it is for Durand's data.

The reappearance of a seasonal in the money market in recent years implies that it is possible to repeat Macaulay's experiment with a new body of data. If the expectations hypothesis is correct, seasonal adjustment factors ought to vary systematically with term to maturity. More specifically, just as the time money rates "anticipated" seasonal changes in call money rates, changes in, say, sixty-day seasonal adjustment factors ought to "anticipate" changes in thirty-day factors. Hence it should be possible to construct a set of seasonal adjustment factors for sixty-day rates if the factors for thirty-day rates are known; knowledge of seasonal adjustment factors for thirty-day bills implies knowledge of these factors for bills of longer maturity.

To test this hypothesis, weekly moving seasonal adjustment factors were computed for twenty-seven- and fifty-five-day bills for 1959, 1960, and 1961, using bid prices unadjusted for bankers discount. If the expectations hypothesis is correct, a set of seasonal adjustment factors for fifty-five-day bills constructed out of twenty-seven-day factors ought to be more strongly correlated with actual fifty-five-day factors than just twenty-seven-day factors alone. For every week, a simple average of twenty-seven-day factors for that week and for four weeks in the future was computed. This should be, according to the expectations hypothesis, a fifty-five-day seasonal. The correlation of this set of theoretical seasonal adjustments with actual fifty-five-day adjustment factors was stronger than the correlation between twenty-seven- and fifty-five-day factors. Converse results ought to hold for a fifty-five-day seasonal adjustment constructed out of twenty-seven-day factors, if the adjustment factors are obtained by averaging the current twenty-seven-day seasonal with that of four weeks in the past. This seasonal, when correlated with the fifty-five-day seasonal directly computed, ought to exhibit less correlation than exists for the relationship between twenty-seven- and fifty-five-day factors. Hence the rank ordering of cor-

TABLE 4

COEFFICIENTS OF CORRELATION BETWEEN WEEKLY SEASONAL
FACTORS IN TREASURY BILL RATES,
1959-61

Type of Seasonal Program	Average of 27-Day Seasonals (Current and 4 Weeks Hence) with 55-Day Seasonal	27-Day Seasonal with 55-Day Seasonal	Average of 27-Day Seasonals (Current and 4-Weeks Past) with 55-Day Seasonal
Multiplicative	.844	.811	.520
Additive	.804	.750	.486

relations alone, quite apart from the question of whether or not there is a significant difference between the correlations, constitutes evidence that the market anticipates seasonal movements in rates. These findings are summarized in Table 4.

The Durand data and the data collected for this study provide a means for discriminating between expectations and liquidity preference on the one hand and market segmentation on the other. The market segmentation hypothesis implies that differences in maturity account for differences in substitutability between securities. If maturity differences are held constant, then the substitutability or the cross elasticity of demand ought also to be constant. In contrast, the expectations hypothesis implies that a seven-year security is more like an eight-year security than a one-year security is like a two-year security. The expectations hypothesis implies that the common element in two securities separated by a year in maturity increases monotonically as term to maturity increases.

Similarly, if one accepts the view that liquidity preference varies with the level of rates, then the premium increases as the level of rates increases. Hence, if securities separated by a year in term to maturity are examined, one should expect the common element to increase as term to maturity increases. Because both liquidity preference and expectations have common implications, this test does not discriminate between them. It does, however, produce evidence that must be regarded as discriminating between expectations and liquidity preference on the one hand and market segmentation on the other.

The foregoing tests were performed with two independent sets of data: the Durand data that Meiselman used and yields to maturity, for the latest cycle, read off the yield curve in the *Treasury Bulletin* by a draftsman. The test employed was a simple rank test. The expectations and liquidity preference hypotheses imply that the correlations between securities separated by a year in term to maturity ought to decrease monotonically as term to maturity increases. Hence the theory forecasts a set of ranks that can be compared with the observed ranks to see if they are positively correlated.

Consistent results were obtained using these independent sets of data. The ranks predicted by the expectations and liquidity preference hypotheses and the actual ranks were highly correlated. Each set of data consisted of nine pairs of ranks. Using the Olds rank correlation test, and interpreting the implications of the liquidity preference and expectations as implying a one-tail test, both significance levels were under 2 per cent.[32]

The foregoing analysis of the implications of liquidity preference and expectations for the correlation between the yields of securities separated by a constant time span as term to maturity increases also implies that yield curves ought to flatten out with maturity. Given that the weights assigned to marginal rates of interest, in the determination of average or internal rates of return, decrease with maturity, then yield curves must flatten out with maturity. This assumes that the variance in forward rates is independent of term to maturity.

The evidence presented supports the Hicksian theory of the term structure of interest rates; it supports the view that both expectations and liquidity preference determine the term structure of interest rates. These results show that forward rates should be interpreted as expected rates plus a liquidity premium. If forward rates are so interpreted, then the expectations of the market seem to forecast subsequently observed short-maturity spot rates; the relationship between expected and subsequently observed spot rates cannot be rationalized as the workings of chance.

With respect to the market segmentation hypothesis, the evidence is less clear. These findings show that this hypothesis is not of the same magnitude as liquidity preference and expectations in the determination of the term structure of rates. The fact that forward rates embody short-term forecasts of spot rates that have a perceptible degree of accuracy implies that liquidity premiums are stable. Hence the scope for the impact of market segmentation upon the term structure of rates must be limited. The Meiselman findings on the relationship between what he termed forecast revisions and errors support this view, as do the tests presented here.

---

[32] The test employed is described in W. Allen Wallis, "Rough-and-Ready Statistical Tests," *Industrial Quality Control*, March, 1952.

A proponent of market segmentation may argue that these tests, in particular, the test based on holding absolute maturity differences constant while varying relative maturity differences, are based on incorrect interpretations of market segmentation. Economic literature does not contain a statement of the market segmentation hypothesis that is as rigorous as those available either for liquidity preference or expectations. Therefore, the possibility of misinterpretation cannot be easily dismissed. The Walker findings which deal with the root of the market segmentation hypothesis are particularly relevant. He showed that institutions have sharply changed the maturity composition of their holdings in response to market forces. This seems to strike at the very foundation of the market segmentation thesis. The only contrary evidence uncovered—this is also subject to the same uncertainties about its relevance—is the existence of negative forward rates in the bill market. Such occurrences seem to be rare, and therefore relatively insignificant, but should not be dismissed entirely. There is always the possibility that more of such evidence exists or that the effects of market segmentation are relatively subtle and the tests employed too crude to detect its existence.[33]

[33] There were negative forward rates in the bill market in the 1930's. At that time rates were relatively low and taxes on bank deposits in Illinois were high enough to make it profitable to take a negative yield rather than be subject to taxation on deposits.

2

WHY LIQUIDITY PREFERENCE EXISTS

IT IS CLEAR from the analysis of the data used by Hickman and Meiselman and the evidence presented here (the historical data going back to 1920 in the next chapter and the comparisons of predicted and actual bill rates), that the expectations hypothesis alone does not explain the term structure of interest rates. The existence of upward bias in the estimates of future short-term rates suggests that at least one other variable is relevant—liquidity preference. Liquidity preference can be regarded as a force that causes forward rates to be biased and high estimates of short-term rates. Its effects can be measured by the difference between the mean value of forward and expected rates; i.e., by the difference between actual forward rates and the yields that short-term securities would have to have for the expectations hypothesis to yield unbiased estimates of future short-term rates. This raises the questions why does liquidity preference exist and how does it affect the term structure of interest rates?

Keynes, who introduced the term to economics, used liquidity preference to describe a preference of the market, abstracting from differences in yield, for assets that are immune to capital losses produced by interest rate changes. If uncertainity as to the future course of interest rates exists, then the market has a choice of taking risks with respect to capital values, income streams, or some combination of both. On balance, the evidence indicates that the market prefers to take risks of income stream changes. That is, the market prefers money to securities if differences in pecuniary yields are ignored.[1] Consequently, equalizing yield differentials exist be-

<hr>

[1] See J. M. Keynes, *The General Theory of Employment, Interest and Money*, New York, 1936, pp. 168 ff. This view may also be found in Hicks, *Value and Capital*, p. 151.

tween money and securities that offset differences in relative vulnerability to capital losses through interest rate changes. Since the risk
of capital losses attributable to holding securities is directly related
to term to maturity, security yields ought also to vary directly with
term to maturity. Just as the "interest rate" equilibrates the net return to holding money and "securities," the term structure of interest rates equilibrates the net return to holding securities of varying terms to maturity and money. The shorter the term to maturity
of a security, the smaller is its vulnerability to capital loss, and
hence the greater its liquidity and the smaller the yield differential
between that security and money. Therefore, liquidity preference
constitutes, by implication, a theory of the term structure of interest rates. It is a theory, not of the level of interest, but of interest
differentials. Linked with risk avoidance, it implies a positively
sloped yield curve.[2]

Short maturities, in addition to being less vulnerable to capital
losses attributable to interest rate changes, have lower costs of con-
version to cash than long maturities. Since the cost of converting
securities to cash increases with term to maturity, the liquidity of
securities, in this specialized sense, decreases with term to maturity.
Consequently, the market ought to prefer short- to long-term securities. Like risk avoidance, transactions costs imply a rising yield
curve as a function of term to maturity. Given the existence of this
inverse relationship, is it strong enough to account for the normal
difference in yields between long- and short-term governments?
Over the three latest reference cycles, the average yield of the long-
est-term governments has been about one hundred basis points
greater than the average yield of 91-day Treasury bills.[3] For three-

2 This view of liquidity preference appears in David W. Lusher, "The Structure of Interest Rates and the Keynesian Theory of Interest," *Journal of Political Economy*, April 1942, p. 274. He says: "Each rate of interest in the structure
of rates may be looked upon as balancing the advantages of holding cash."
Similarly, Abba P. Lerner in *Economics of Control*, New York, 1944, p. 343,
says: "Competition equalizes the *sum* of money and liquidity yields." Samuelson
regards liquidity preference as an explanation of the existence and level, not of
the interest rate, but of the differential between the yield on money and the
yields on other assets. See Paul A. Samuelson, *Foundations of Economic Analysis*,
Vol. 80, Harvard Economic Studies, Cambridge, Mass., 1947, pp. 122–124.

3 If the first postwar cycle (October 1945 to October 1949) is included in this
calculation, a greater average spread between bills and long-term governments

month Treasury bills, turnaround costs (that is, the costs of getting
into and out of bills) typically are around one-sixty-fourth of 1 per
cent of value at maturity, or about sixteen cents.[4] In contrast, corresponding costs for the longest of long-term governments are about
eight-thirty-seconds, or $2.50. Insofar as bills are bought at the
weekly auction and held to maturity, transactions costs for their
holders are zero. If bills are bought at auction and not held to
maturity, or if bought from a dealer and held to maturity, then
the relevant transactions costs are about eight cents. Bonds can,
of course, also be bought directly from the Treasury and held to
maturity. However, bonds are sold by the Treasury relatively infrequently, and infrequently held to maturity.

The extent to which transactions costs can account for the observed difference in yields on three-month bills and longer maturities is a function of the holding period. In general, the longer the
holding period, the less the relative disadvantage of longer maturities, and conversely. If bills and long-term bonds are compared for
a holding period of three months, and if bills are bought at auction
and held to maturity and long-term bonds are bought and sold
through a dealer, then the equalizing yield differential is equivalent
to 1 per cent per year. That is, 4 per cent is the net yield to the

---

results. The average size of the bill-bond spread is larger for the first than for
any of the three succeeding cycles. It is excluded on the grounds that the bill rate
for most of the first postwar cycle was largely a fictitious rate. The governmental policy that stabilized the prewar term structure of interest rates led to a bill
yield that was low relative to the yield on bonds. The reduction in the size of
the bill-bond spread between the first and the succeeding postwar cycles constitutes additional evidence that the reported bill rate was out of line with the
yield on long-term governments and was, in effect, a nominal rate.

[4] The Commission on Money and Credit in their report, *Money and Credit*,
Englewood Cliffs, New Jersey, 1961, p. 118, attributes the higher transactions costs
to the greater risks to dealers of trading in long-term governments. This explanation implies that these costs must have been lower during the period when the
structure of interest rates was pegged. In fact, the spreads between bid and
asked prices were about half of what they are now.

Dealer operations are highly leveraged, more so than those of most banks, and
the value of government securities as collateral is inversely related to term to
maturity. The Joint Economic Committee, *A Study of the Dealer Market for
Federal Government Securities*, Washington, D.C., 1960, p. 92, reports that dealer
margin requirements for Treasury bills are one-quarter of 1 per cent. They are
one-half of 1 per cent for certificates, 1 per cent for bonds under five years,
2 per cent for bonds between five and ten years to maturity, and 3 per cent for
maturities over ten years.

holder of long-term governments, if the yield to maturity is 5 per cent; 3 per cent is the net yield, if the yield to maturity is 4 per cent, etc.[5] This implies that an investor who calculates on an expected value basis, and who wants to invest for three months and assumes that the yields of long-term securities will average 1 per cent more than bills, will find no difference between bills and long-term governments. Consequently, for holding periods less than three months, the equalizing yield spread between bills and bonds is in excess of an annual rate of 1 per cent. For more than three months, it is less than 1 per cent. For six months, the equalizing yield differential on an annual basis is one-half of 1 per cent, and for one year, one-quarter of 1 per cent.

If one assumes transactions costs for bills of one-thirty-second, which is a more realistic assumption, the equalizing yield differential between bills and nine- to twelve-month governments for a three-month holding period is twelve to thirteen basis points (this assumes a two-thirty-second turnaround cost for the longer maturity). When nine- to twelve-month governments are compared with three- to five-year governments for a one-year holding period, the equalizing yield differential is about six basis points (this assumes a two-thirty-second turnaround cost for the shorter, and a four-thirty-second cost for the longer maturity).

Actual yield differentials (implied by Table 7) have exceeded the equalizing yield differentials computed above. This suggests that pure transactions costs do not fully account for the observed yield differentials. However, one must be careful in making this comparison. During the period encompassed by Table 7, there was a secular trend upward in yields which caused holders of long-term securities to incur capital losses. Therefore, for the long bond-bill comparison, it is necessary to add the assumption that the market failed to anticipate the secular rise in rates.[6]

[5] A $2.50 transaction cost would come to $10.00 on an annual basis, hence it would reduce the gross yield by 10/1000, or 1 per cent.

[6] This assumption is consistent with a number of other observations. It is consistent with the observed difference between correlations of forward and one-year spot rates considered for just one cycle and for the entire 1901–54 period when a secular downward movement was followed by a secular upward movement in rates. It is consistent with the finding that the differential between bills and nine- to twelve-month governments cannot be explained by transactions cost

On the whole, this analysis suggests that yield differentials as a function of term to maturity cannot be rationalized completely as a consequence of transactions cost differences. Risk avoidance must be introduced. Unfortunately this statement and the calculations upon which it is based are not as straightforward as they appear. Typically, bid and asked prices overstate spreads; most transactions take place within this range and almost none outside of it. This tends to make the advantage of investing in long-term securities somewhat better than these calculations indicate. On the other hand, because the market for long-term governments is relatively thinner than that for short-term governments, the price at which a transaction takes place is more likely to be affected by its size. As a result, more transactions in long-term governments are brokerage transactions than is true of bills. Virtually all bills are bought and sold for the account and risk of dealers, whereas for long-term governments, dealers less frequently buy and sell from their own inventories for their customers.[7] Hence, an estimated 25 per cent of all trading in long-term governments represents brokerage transactions. From the point of view of the holders of long-term securities, this alone makes them less liquid than bills because it takes more time to consummate a brokerage transaction than a dealer

---

differences alone. For this comparison, trends in rates are virtually irrelevant. And finally, it is consistent with the composite yield curve for 1901–54 implied by the Durand data. The difference between the average yields of long- and short-term securities cannot be explained by transactions costs. Yet on balance, the trend in interest rates for this entire period is, if anything, down.

[7] This seems to be a direct result of a thin market. Dealers that expect long-term bond prices to fall would be willing to buy all offered for their own account if they could either turn around and sell them at the existing market price or sell short another issue very similar to the issue offered. To the extent that hedging is possible, dealers can win trading profits without incurring risks of capital losses. Since only three or four dealers deal extensively in long-term governments, it is not unusual to find that they all have the same price expectations. If they expect a fall in prices, they are willing to buy at current prices only what it is possible to hedge; they will buy the rest only at less than current price.

Bid and asked prices widen when prices are expected to fall and narrow when they are expected to rise as a result of changes in the cost of carrying inventories. Of course, quoted bid and asked prices often are not meaningful numbers when dealers are unwilling to take positions.

Brokerage costs for a complete turnaround, a purchase and a sale, are usually two-thirty-seconds or less. However, would-be brokerage transactions are subject to the risk of never being consummated. They make sense when customer market expectations differ from those of dealers.

trade. Most of the time, and for most transactions, the difference between bid and asked prices for bills and long-term bonds measures the relative costs of transactions. For large transactions, however, say over two million (which would be regarded as a small transaction in bills), bonds are substantially less liquid than bills when dealers expect yields to rise. Hence, bid and asked prices with the usual spreads understate the relative costs of trading in the long-term bonds.[8]

Although ambiguities exist in the measurement of transactions costs for long-term securities, it seems fairly clear that average yield differentials as a function of term to maturity, if cyclical effects upon yield differentials are ignored, are too large to be solely explained by transactions costs. Hence, the Keynesian view, that short-term securities are preferred in order to avoid risks of capital losses, does have a role to play in explaining observed yield differentials. Motives other than transactions costs must be introduced to explain the observed yield differentials; the rationale for the holding of money substitutes is the same as the rationale for the holding of money proper.

The Keynesian view of the term structure of interest rates has implications that are, in a crude sense, consistent with observed yield differentials over the cycle. This view does more than imply that yield curves ought to rise with term to maturity. Vulnerability to capital loss is not a linear function of term to maturity; it increases at a decreasing rate with increases in maturity. Hence average yields ought to rise with term to maturity at a decreasing rate. To illustrate: an unanticipated permanent increase in short-term rates from 3 to 6 per cent implies, for securities bearing a 3 per cent coupon, that (a) a perpetuity would lose half its value, (b) a bond with a twelve-year term to maturity would fall in value by 25 per cent, and (c) a bond with four years to maturity would fall in value by about 10 per cent.[9]

---

[8] There is a danger of making too much of this point. It is clear that the market for long-term governments is characterized by a larger volume of trading than the most heavily traded corporate security, A. T. & T. bonds.

[9] This point appears in Harry C. Sauvain, "Changing Interest Rates and the Investment Portfolio," *Journal of Finance*, May 1959, pp. 235 ff., and Malkiel, *Quarterly Journal of Economics*, May 1962, p. 202, theorem 3.
These authors fail to point out that the greater variance in the prices of long-

The evidence for postwar business cycles shows that average yields rise at a decreasing rate as term to maturity increases. For the three latest cycles, the spread between bills and nine- to twelve-month governments is thirty basis points. This implies a rise in the average rate, for this segment of the yield curve, of about forty-eight basis points per year. The yield spread between nine- to twelve-month governments and three- to five-year governments is forty-three basis points, or a rise in the average rate of about seventeen basis points per year. The differential in yields between three- to five-year governments and twenty-year governments is twenty-eight basis points. Hence the average rate for the segment encompassed by these two maturities rises about one and three-quarter basis points a year. Similar conclusions are implied by the composite yield curve constructed from Durand's data [10] (see Chart 2).

The Keynesian view, that the market prefers short- to long-term securities to avoid the risks of capital losses, does not imply that participants in this market need be characterized as risk avoiders generally. An enterprise that is quite willing to speculate in what it regards as its principal line of economic activity may rationally be unwilling to run risks of capital losses on its holdings of money substitutes. As long as it can speculate more efficiently in its principal activities, there is no inconsistency between its risk aversion in bond markets and risk acceptance or preference in other markets.

This argument is symmetrical for money holders. Some money is held in preference to long- and short-term governments to avoid risk. Yet it does not follow that money holders are generally risk avoiders. To determine whether they are or not involves an over-all

term vis-à-vis those of short-term bonds is an economic, and not an arithmetic, proposition which rests on the assumption that errors in forecasting future spot rates are positively correlated. In principle, prices of long-term bonds could fluctuate less than short-term bonds. To illustrate: Consider the price behavior of a one- and a two-year bond, assuming that errors in forecasting the current one-year rate are negatively correlated with errors in forecasting the one-year rate one year hence. If long-term bonds did not fluctuate in price more than short-term bonds, then Meiselman would not have observed that forecasting errors and forecast revisions were positively correlated.

[10] Malkiel (ibid., p. 206) also concludes that, as term to maturity increases, yield curves flatten out and the marginal vulnerability to interest rate changes decreases.

evaluation of their total risk positions. Knowledge of just money holdings, or money substitute holdings, is not enough.[11]

Acceptance of the Keynesian empirical judgment that the market for governments is largely composed of risk avoiders does not necessarily imply that short-term rates will be systematically lower than long-term rates. It suggests that speculative opportunities will exist for those who are willing to bear risks, i.e., those who are willing to calculate on an expected value basis. More specifically, it suggests that there ought to exist gains to be derived from being short on near maturities and long on distant maturities.[12]

Such a financing short is rarely undertaken. The going rate for borrowing securities is one-half of 1 per cent. This is, in effect, a call loan rate for governments. It can be terminated at the option of either the supplier of securities on loan or the borrower. Securities on loan usually can be recalled on twenty-four hours notice. Borrowers of securities must maintain collateral, in the form of other governments, with the lenders of securities. The borrower usually has the right to substitute from day to day among the securities held as collateral, subject to the constraint that the aggregate value of the collateral be equal to or greater than the securities borrowed.[13] The short seller must, when the lender wants his securities back, either arrange for another loan or close out his short position. In any case, he must reacquire the securities initially borrowed through a new loan or by buying them in the market. Since bills are held as money substitutes, the calling up of borrowed bills by lenders during their term to maturity is to be expected. Insofar as longer-term securities than bills are borrowed, the trans-

[11] Similarly, the fact that a firm holds cash balances does not imply that it is a creditor and is expecting deflation. Nor does the existence of bonds outstanding for a firm imply that it is a net debtor. A more complex analysis of the entire structure of monetary assets and monetary liabilities is necessary before such a judgment can be reached.

[12] It is important to recognize that this is not arbitrage. Changes in interest rates will produce dramatic effects on the net equity position of a speculator in such a position. A rise in rates implies capital losses, and a fall, capital gains.

[13] This is one of the principal factors that make the loan rate as high as one-half of 1 per cent. The lenders of securities, usually banks, incur clerical costs as a result of frequent changes in the collateral offered by borrowers, typically government bond dealers. Bond dealers usually offer the securities held in their position as collateral.

actions costs for borrowing and reborrowing are reduced at the expense of higher rates of interest. Consequently, the short seller has the choice of costs in the form of low interest rates (i.e., the yields of very short maturities) with borrowing and reborrowing problems, or somewhat higher rates and somewhat more stable borrowing arrangements.[14]

The costs of maintaining and financing a short position are usually so large that it is more economical for dealers to finance the holding of long-term governments through bank loans or repurchase agreements. As a consequence, the yields of short-term securities are brought into line with long-term yields, not directly through a short position in near-term maturities, but indirectly through borrowing in the money market (i.e., a short position in bank credit). For the suppliers of funds for the money market— banks and nonfinancial institutions such as industrial enterprises— providing credit to dealers is an alternative to holding bills. Consequently, the bill rate is linked to the cost of short-term dealer financing through both the demand and the supply side of the market. As a result of this interrelationship between the yield on long-term governments on the one hand and financing costs of dealers in the money market on the other, an equilibrium spread exists between the yields of short- and long-term governments. In equilibrium, the marginal costs of borrowing to finance the holding of long-term governments should equal the yield spread between bills and bonds. This spread measures the marginal costs of the resources required for additional commitments in long-term securities financed by short-term liabilities.

Insofar as costs of speculating on the spreads between bills and bonds exist, speculation will not operate to make the expected value of bond yields the same as bill yields. Bonds will yield more than bills and this differential will be a function of the costs of being short on near maturities and long on distant maturities. That such positive costs exist is strongly supported by the empirical evidence. Their existence implies that forward rates implicit in the

[14] Joint Economic Committee, *Study of the Dealer Market*, p. 59, reports that the probability of a transaction in a government security is inversely related to its term to maturity.

term structure of interest rates, if one accepts the expectations hypothesis, will be biased estimates of future short-term rates. The interesting question is, how large are the costs of simultaneously taking long positions on distant maturities and short positions on near maturities?

The government bond market does not exist in isolation. At the short end it is an integral part of the money market, and at the long end, of the capital market. A number of financial institutions (in particular, commercial banks, the Federal Reserve System, savings banks, investment banks, savings and loan associations, life insurance companies, government, municipal, and corporate bond dealers, and the Federal National Mortgage Association), although conventionally regarded as being extremely conservative, are speculators in the money and capital markets. The average maturity of their assets is greater than the average maturity of their nonequity liabilities. Hence, they are speculators in the sense that they are long on long-term money and short on short-term money and by and large, live on the carry. Their economic viability is a function of the spread in yields between their assets and their liabilities.

Each of these classes of financial institutions operates in distinct and overlapping portions of the money and capital markets. Moreover, the specifics of their modus operandi differ. Savings banks, savings and loan associations, and life insurance companies issue forms of time deposits to finance their acquisition of assets. Commercial banks and the Federal Reserve Banks hold many short-term assets, but they issue demand deposits. Dealers and investment bankers use bank loans and similar short-term credit instruments; life insurance companies hold extremely long-term assets. These institutions all operate the same way in one essential respect—they reduce the yields on long maturities and raise the yields on short maturities. The existence of an average yield differential between bills and bonds of about one hundred basis points over the three latest reference cycles reflects the marginal costs of speculation to reduce this yield differential. It emerges despite the work of all of these financial institutions and reflects the fact that speculative activity, like most economic activities, is not cost free.

This analysis suggests that there exists an equalizing difference in yields between short- and long-term governments. This yield differential measures, at the margin, the relative advantages of short- and long-term governments as money substitutes, i.e., as a means of avoiding risks of interest rate changes and keeping down transactions costs. It is analytically the same as the yield differential between cash and long-term bonds that is often referred to as "the rate of interest," but it is smaller because short-term governments are less than perfect substitutes for cash balances.

The analysis also suggests that the spread between long- and short-term governments need not be the same as the spread between long- and short-term corporate bonds. Corporates have higher trans-actions costs which limit the value of short-term corporates as money substitutes. Hence, the corporate short-long spread ought to be smaller than the corresponding yield spread for governments. The usual brokerage charge for buying and selling a corporate bond that is listed on the New York Stock Exchange and sells for about $1,000 is $5.00, or one-half of 1 per cent. However, there is some question as to whether the cost is comparable to the spread between the bid and asked prices for governments. The latter in-cludes the cost of the services of the dealer who takes a position, whereas the former does not. A more relevant comparison is the over-the-counter, one-hundred bond corporate market. This is where most bonds are bought and sold. Dealers take positions and have buying and selling prices comparable to the bid and asked price for governments. For the bonds of A. T. & T., the corporate security with the widest market, the most frequently found spread is three-quarters, or $7.50 per bond for long-term bonds. This ranges down to about one-sixteenth for the very shortest-term bonds.

These findings strongly support the Keynesian theory of "normal backwardation" which rests on the premise that speculative services on net balance come at a positive pecuniary cost to society. This theory has common implications for commodity markets and the markets for government securities.[15] In commodity markets, the

15 John M. Keynes, *A Treatise on Money*, Vol. II: *The Applied Theory of Money*, London, 1930, pp. 142 ff. This theory also appears in Hicks, *Value and Capital*, pp. 136 ff.

theory implies that forward prices are biased and low estimates of future spot prices; the prices of forward commitments rise as their term to maturity shortens. Similarly, in the money and capital markets, the theory implies that forward rates are biased and high estimates of spot rates; the prices of forward commitments rise as their term to maturity shortens.

Normal backwardation views speculators as selling insurance services to risk avoiders (or hedgers, in the case of commodity markets). This particular type of insurance, in common with insurance generally, comes at a cost to society; the nonpecuniary returns to speculators as a class are not large enough to compensate them for the opportunity costs of the resources used to provide their services. In contrast to this view, Professor Knight and, subsequently, Professor Telser enunciated the view that hedgers or risk avoiders provide the services of a casino to speculators.[16] Futures markets, in their view, are places where a speculator or gambler can get relatively favorable betting odds, i.e., where the house take is relatively small. Consequently, they contend that forward prices could represent unbiased or even high estimates of the spot value of future commitments. The nonpecuniary returns to speculators can be large enough to compensate or more than compensate for the opportunity costs of the resources employed in providing speculative services.

These views of futures markets imply that individuals choose either to bear risks or to hire speculators to bear risks, at either positive, zero, or negative cost. In fact the choice confronting the holders of governments is either to bear risks of capital losses or risks of income instability, or some combination of both. Given the stocks of long- and short-term securities that have been outstanding during the period under investigation, society has on balance chosen to bear the risks of income uncertainty and to hire speculators at positive costs to bear the risks of capital uncertainty.[17]

[16] Frank H. Knight, *The Economic Organization*, New York, 1951, p. 79; Lester G. Telser, "Reply," *Journal of Political Economy*, August 1960, p. 406.

[17] Although society has, on balance, paid for the service of bearing the risk of capital losses, this does not imply that those who have provided this service have been unable to hedge their risks. Insurance companies, because of the predictability of their expenditures, have been important suppliers of this service. Commonly, authors have referred to insurance company liabilities as long term. It is

The costs of bearing the risks of income uncertainty appear to have been negative. If "normal backwardation" is interpreted to mean avoiding the risk of capital losses and not risk avoidance per se, then these findings support the Keynesian view.[18]

The existence of bias in the estimates of future short-term rates, implied by the Lutz-Meiselman variant of the expectations hypothesis, implies that securities of different terms to maturity are not perfect substitutes for one another when the holding period yields are equal. The existence of positive costs of arbitrage and speculation is a necessary condition for the existence of liquidity premiums. Whether there exists any yield relationship for which securities of different maturities are perfect substitutes depends on the character of cost conditions in the production of speculative services.

The evidence presented suggests that the futures market for money is in a sense segmented into many markets that are partly isolated from one another through the existence of costs of converting long- into short-term securities. This market, like that for beer in the United States, is segmented by the existence of transportation costs.[19]

---

clear that these liabilities are not long term in the same sense that the issuer of a long-term bond has a long-term liability. The cash surrender value of an insurance policy is clearly a short-term liability, as are the rights to borrow against cash surrender values. Similarly, death benefits may be regarded as constrained short-term liabilities.

[18] The empirical evidence that has been brought to bear on the issue of bias in forward rates in commodity markets has not been interpreted as providing clear support for either the Knightian or Keynesian position. In large part, the source of the difficulty has been that a very small bias in forward prices could provide the going rate of return on capital to speculators. Yet the presence of a small bias, particularly in a world in which prices have not been absolutely stable, is very hard to detect. The relevant literature on this point includes Lester G. Telser, "Futures Trading and the Storage of Cotton and Wheat," *Journal of Political Economy*, June 1958, p. 233; a subsequent exchange between Cootner and Telser in the August 1960 issue of the same journal; and Holbrook Working, "New Concepts Concerning Futures Markets and Prices," *American Economic Review*, June 1962, pp. 449–454.

[19] Specialists in the market for government securities are fond of arguing that no one regards long- and short-term securities as perfect substitutes for one another (presumably when holding period yields are alike), hence they are not perfect substitutes in the market. Although this reasoning leaves something to be desired, the conclusion appears to be valid.

A striking piece of evidence, already cited, that corroborates the views of

The introduction of costs of converting long- into short-term securities implies that, if the provision of speculative services in this market is an increasing cost industry, the relative yields of short- and long-term securities can be affected by the maturity composition of outstanding stocks. Hence, these yields can be influenced by open market operations; whether or not the Fed (Federal Reserve System) follows a bills-only policy can make a difference. Insofar as the Fed buys bills, and bills only, the decrease in the stock of bills outstanding implies an increase in the volume of speculative services produced by financial intermediaries and hence a rise in yield differentials. Conversely, insofar as the Fed buys only long-term governments, the decrease in the stock of these securities outstanding implies a decrease in the volume of speculative services produced by financial intermediaries and hence a fall in yield differentials. How large this fall or rise will be depends upon the supply elasticity of speculative services.

Increasing costs of providing speculative services imply that variations in the stocks of long- and short-term governments outstanding will affect long-short yield differentials. This is a sufficient but not a necessary condition for open market operations to affect yield curves. The existence of constant costs for speculative services implies that a specified range of yield differentials will exist; this range will be analogous to gold points under a gold standard. Depending upon how wide the counterparts to gold points are, there still remains some scope for open market operations as a means of influencing the long-short yield differential. Probably the strongest grounds for believing that increasing costs are relevant is the argu-

market practitioners is the term structure of bill yields during September 1960. These observations show that positive costs of arbitrage must exist. Hence, by an a fortiori argument, positive costs of providing speculative services must also exist. Assuming that the market prefers to avoid risks of capital loss, these costs imply a positively sloped yield curve. The rarely observed negative forward rates were produced apparently by corporate treasurers who, to meet tax obligations on December 15, mechanically bought Treasury bills that matured on December 15 in order to match tax expenditures with receipts.

The existence of these costs of arbitrage or speculation implies that forward rates can vary from expected rates. Forward rates are usually higher than expected rates and the difference can be accounted for by risk avoidance and speculative costs. Insofar as this is what is meant by market segmentation, the position of specialists in the market is correct.

ment that there exist variations among investors with respect to their willingness to bear risk. Hence, as the volume of speculative services produced increases, the costs of financial resources to speculators will also increase.

A theoretical frame of reference similar to that enunciated in this section seems to be implicit in the writings of many economists in the field of debt management. For example, Simons believed that short-term debt is a better money substitute than long-term debt.[20] This implies that there must be a pecuniary yield differential between long- and short-term debt since aggregate or total yield on both types of debt must be equal. Hence, a positively sloped yield curve is implied.[21] An advocate of a pure expectations hypothesis would regard short- and long-term debt as having equal inflationary potential; variations in the maturity distribution of outstanding debt would have no effect on aggregate demand.

[20] See "On Debt Management," and "Rules Versus Authorities in Monetary Policy," in Henry C. Simons, *Economic Policy for a Free Society*, Chicago, 1948.
[21] Simons (*ibid.*, p. 225) recognizes this implication when he says, ". . . issue-yields will normally vary directly with maturities."

HOW SHORT- AND LONG-TERM
INTEREST RATES
HAVE BEHAVED CYCLICALLY

THE BEHAVIOR of the term structure of interest rates during business cycles can be summarized by:

1. Relative yields of short- and long-term securities at cycle peaks and troughs.
2. Variance in yields over the cycle as a function of term to maturity.
3. Average yields over the cycle as a function of term to maturity.
4. Correspondence of peaks and troughs in yields with business cycle peaks and troughs.

In the first part of this chapter, the behavior of the term structure of interest rates since the end of World War II is described. Then the yields on government securities during the period between the two world wars are examined. Finally, the cyclical variation and relative level of yields on long- and short-term nongovernmental obligations since 1858 is reviewed.

Since the end of World War II, there have been pronounced specific cycles in interest-rate series. The peaks and troughs of these series have been closely associated with turning points in business conditions. For the first four complete business cycles following the war, intra-cyclical changes in interest rates were, on the average, 50 per cent greater than cycle-to-cycle changes. Although there was a strong trend upward in interest rates during this time, peak-to-trough and trough-to-peak changes in rates were large relative to secular changes (see Table 5).

Relative to secular trends, peak-to-trough changes in short maturities were especially large. From the trough in the earliest of

TABLE 5

CYCLICAL CHANGES IN YIELDS OF GOVERNMENT SECURITIES,
OCTOBER 1945–FEBRUARY 1961[a]

Business Cycle			Absolute Values (per cent)			Changes	
Trough	Peak	Trough	Trough	Peak	Trough	Trough to Peak	Peak to Trough
A. Three-month Treasury bills							
10/45	11/48	10/49	.38	1.12	1.05	.74	-.07
10/49	7/53	8/54	1.05	2.10	.88	1.05	-1.22
8/54	7/57	4/58	.88	3.59	1.16	2.71	-2.43
4/58	5/60	2/61	1.16	3.53	2.29	2.37	-1.24
B. Nine- to twelve-month governments							
10/45	11/48	10/49	.82	1.21	1.08	.39	-.13
10/49	7/53	8/54	1.08	2.40	.62	1.32	-1.78
8/54	7/57	4/58	.62	3.89	1.40	3.27	-2.49
4/58	5/60	2/61	1.40	4.32	2.79	2.92	-1.53
C. Three- to five-year governments							
10/45	11/48	10/49	1.15	1.67	1.36	.52	-.31
10/49	7/53	8/54	1.36	2.74	1.68	1.38	-1.06
8/54	7/57	4/58	1.68	3.95	2.41	2.27	-1.54
4/58	5/60	2/61	2.41	4.63	3.52	2.22	-1.11
D. Twenty-year governments							
10/45	11/48	10/49	2.07	2.42	2.20	.35	-.22
10/49	7/53	8/54	2.20	3.09	2.52	.89	-.57
8/54	7/57	4/58	2.52	3.62	3.11	1.10	-.51
4/58	5/60	2/61	3.11	4.24	3.77	1.13	-.47
Averages, Four Cycles, 1945-61							
Three-month Treasury bills						1.72	-1.24
Nine- to twelve-month governments						1.98	-1.48
Three- to five-year governments						1.60	-1.00
Twenty-year governments						.87	-.44

Source: Series are adjusted for seasonal variation by the National
Bureau. All series, except the twenty-year government bond series, are
compiled by the Federal Reserve Board and are reported monthly in the
Federal Reserve Bulletin. The twenty-year government bond series is
compiled by the Morgan Guaranty Trust Co.

[a] During this time, there was a half cycle of experience with six-month
Treasury bills. For this half cycle, May 1960 through February 1961, 182-
day bills decreased from 3.58 to 2.60, a change of 98 basis points. (A
basis point is equal to .01 per cent.)

The three-month bill series is, strictly speaking, not directly comparable with the other series. Yields of bills are discount yields based
on a 360-day, and not the usual 365-day year. Hence, bill yields understate correct yields, and the true yield differentials between bills and
other securities is less than the differences reported here. In general,
the higher the absolute level of bill rates, the greater the bias. For
bill yields of 2.5 to 3 per cent, the bias is around eight basis points.

these four cycles to the trough in the latest, a period of more than fifteen years, interest-rate changes for bills and nine- to twelve-month governments were less than the trough-to-peak changes in the two latest cycles.

Since the trough-to-peak increases in short-term rates were greater than the corresponding increases in long-term rates, the former rose relative to the latter during expansions. Conversely, short-term rates fell relatively during contractions, since their peak-to-trough decreases were greater. Consequently, short-term rates were relatively high about cyclical peaks and low about troughs.

The relative changes in short- and long-term yields over the cycle imply systematic changes in yield differentials or spreads between maturity classes. Since short-term rates were typically below long-term rates, spreads between them narrowed during the course of an expansion and widened during a contraction. Absolute differences became smaller when rates increased and larger when rates decreased. For the three latest cycles (1949–61), an absolute increase in bill yields of one-hundred basis points was associated with an average decrease in the spread between bills and twenty-year government bonds of forty-three basis points.[1]

This evidence also indicates that short-term rates were more variable absolutely over the cycle (see Table 6). However, the general belief that the longer the term to maturity, the less volatile the yield, is not entirely supported. In each of the three latest cycles, nine- to twelve-month governments were more variable absolutely than three-month Treasury bills. This suggests that the absolute variability in yields over the cycle first increased and then decreased with the term to maturity.

In contrast to the spreads between bills and long-term governments, the yield differential between bills and nine- to twelve-month governments widened over the course of the post-World War II expansions and narrowed during the contractions. For the three latest cycles, an absolute increase of 1 per cent in the yields of bills was associated with an average increase of eighteen basis points in the differential.

[1] The slope of the regression equation relating the absolute size of the yield differential between bills and bonds to the absolute level of bill yields was .43.

TABLE 6

VARIATION IN YIELDS OF GOVERNMENT SECURITIES DURING FOUR BUSINESS CYCLES,
OCTOBER 1945–FEBRUARY 1961

Business Cycle, Trough to Trough	Three-Month Bills	Nine- to Twelve-Month Governments	Three- to Five-Year Governments	Twenty-Year Governments
Standard deviation				
10/45 to 10/49	.334	.159	.197	.163
10/49 to 8/54	.375	.434	.405	.259
8/54 to 4/58	.817	.886	.605	.311
4/58 to 2/61	.874	1.031	.698	.321
Coefficient of variation[a]				
10/45 to 10/49	44.59	16.19	14.43	7.40
10/49 to 8/54	25.41	27.45	20.51	10.04
8/54 to 4/58	35.58	35.44	20.78	10.10
4/58 to 2/61	31.87	30.72	18.15	8.22

[a]Standard deviation stated as a percentage of the mean.

TABLE 7

AVERAGE YIELD OF GOVERNMENT SECURITIES DURING FOUR BUSINESS CYCLES,
OCTOBER 1945–FEBRUARY 1961
(per cent)

Business Cycle, Trough to Trough	Three-Month Bills	Nine- to Twelve-Month Governments	Three- to Five-Year Governments	Twenty-Year Governments
10/45 to 10/49	.749	.982	1.365	2.203
10/49 to 8/54	1.476	1.581	1.975	2.580
8/54 to 4/58	2.296	2.500	2.912	3.079
4/58 to 2/61	2.742	3.356	3.846	3.904
Unweighted average of the cycle averages				
10/45 to 2/61	1.816	2.105	2.524	2.942

Unlike the variability in yields over the cycle, average yields varied monotonically with term to maturity (see Table 7). The longer the term to maturity, the higher the yield. This suggests that yield curves were, on the average, positively sloped during the four 1945–61 cycles.[2] Slopes were invariably positive from the end

TABLE 8

TIMING OF SHORT- AND LONG-TERM YIELDS OF GOVERNMENT SECURITIES
AT BUSINESS CYCLE PEAKS AND TROUGHS,
OCTOBER 1945–FEBRUARY 1961

	Lead (−) or Lag (+) in Months, at Business Cycle Peaks and Troughs							
	10/45 T	11/48 P	10/49 T	7/53 P	8/54 T	7/57 P	4/58 T	5/60 P	2/61 T
1. Three-month bills	a	a	a	−1	−2	−1	+2	−5	−2
2. Nine- to twelve-month governments	a	+4	−3	−1	0	0	+2	−4	−1
3. Three- to five-year governments	+5	−3	−3	−1	0	0	+2	−5	−5
4. Twenty-year governments	+4	−1	+2	−1	0	−1	0	−4	−5

[a]No specific cycle.

of the war through 1955, but in more recent years, curves with negatively sloped segments have been observed.

In general, the steepness or the degree to which yield curves were positively inclined decreased from trough-to-peak. Only about peaks could one observe yield curves with negative slopes (see Table 5 and Charts 5 and 6). Negatively sloped yield curves, or more

2 Yield curves depict, at one point in time, average rates of interest as a function of term to maturity. They portray the average yield of securities that are homogeneous with respect to credit-worthiness and vary only in term to maturity. Marginal rate of interest curves bear the same relation to yield curves that marginal cost curves bear to average cost curves. These show marginal rates of interest as a function of term to maturity and are implied by yield curves. A one-to-one correspondence exists between points on marginal rate of interest curves and yield curves. Marginal rate of interest curves are usually referred to as forward rates; they are the incremental or marginal costs of borrowing for two years instead of one year, etc. The marginal cost of extending a one-year maturity for an additional year is the forward rate for one-year money one year hence. Estimates of current yield curves for government securities are reported monthly in the *Treasury Bulletin*.

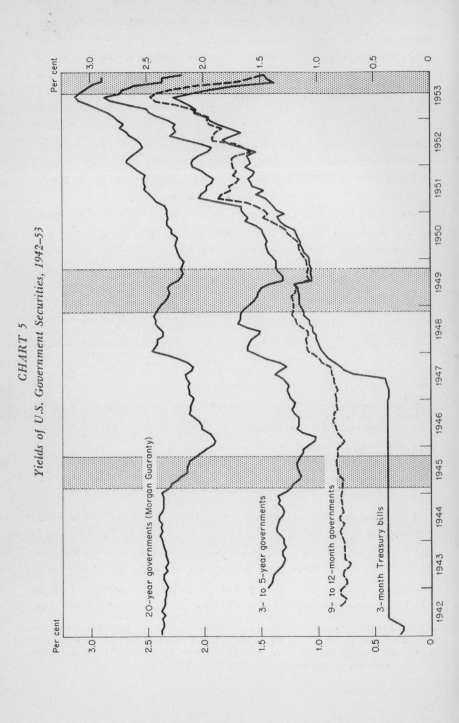

CHART 5

Yields of U.S. Government Securities, 1942–53

Per cent

20-year governments (Morgan Guaranty)

3- to 5-year governments

9- to 12-month governments

3-month Treasury bills

1942 1943 1944 1945 1946 1947 1948 1949 1950 1951 1952 1953

correctly yield curves with negatively sloped segments, occurred about the 1957 and 1960 cyclical peaks.

During the 1945–61 business cycles, the peaks and troughs in the specific cycles of governments were roughly synchronous with those in business activity. For bills, the degree of synchronization is poorest for the earliest cycle and roughly on a par with longer-term governments for the three later cycles (see Table 8, and Charts 5 and 6). The striking coincidence of timing in specific and business cycles suggests that the forces that determine the peaks and troughs of business cycles must also play a role in determining those in the specific cycles of time series of government obligations.[3]

Seasonally adjusting the time series used had relatively little effect on the dating of specific cycle peaks and troughs. If anything the correspondence of specific with business cycle peaks was closer after adjustment (see Table 9).

TABLE 9

TIMING OF PEAKS AND TROUGHS IN BILL RATES USING
SEASONALLY ADJUSTED AND UNADJUSTED DATA

Bill Rates	Business Cycle Turns					
	P	T	P	T	P	T
Unadjusted						
Date of specific cycle turn	4/53	6/54	10/57	6/58	12/59	1/61
Lead (−) or lag (+) in months,						
relative to business cycle turn	−3	−2	+3	+2	−5	−1
Adjusted						
Date of specific cycle turn	6/53	6/54	6/57	6/58	12/59	12/60
Lead (−) or lag (+) in months,						
relative to business cycle turn	−1	−2	−1	+2	−5	−2

The time series upon which these uniformities in the cyclical behavior of interest rates are based appear in Charts 5 and 6. These time series unfortunately do not go back before World War II. In the 1920's and 1930's, the interest on virtually all of the long-term governments outstanding was partially tax exempt, and on short-term governments wholly tax exempt. The issuance of Treas-

---

[3] Of the thirty-two specific cycle turning points, nineteen preceded the corresponding business cycle turning point, seven succeeded, and six were coincidental. On average, specific cycle turning points led by 0.9 months. At peaks, the average lead was 1.6 months; at troughs, 0.3 months.

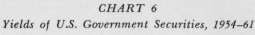

CHART 6

Yields of U.S. Government Securities, 1954–61

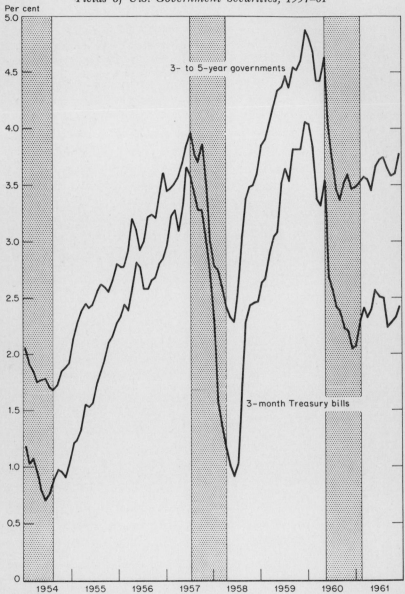

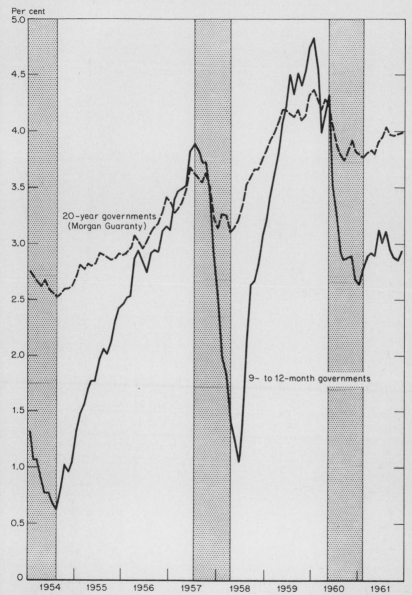

Per cent

20-year governments
(Morgan Guaranty)

9- to 12-month governments

NOTE: Shaded areas represent business cycle contractions; unshaded areas, expansions.

ury bills began in December 1929, but offerings in the following
two years were so infrequent and irregular that a continuous series
does not begin until 1931. Before 1931, yields on short-term governments could be measured by a series on three- to six-month Treasury notes and certificates that began in 1920 and ended in 1933.
The income derived from holding these notes and certificates was
fully tax exempt. In summary, prewar data that depict the relative
yields of short- and long-term governments over the cycle are not
directly comparable to postwar data, and the short-term data for

CHART 7

Yields of U.S. Government Securities, 1920–33

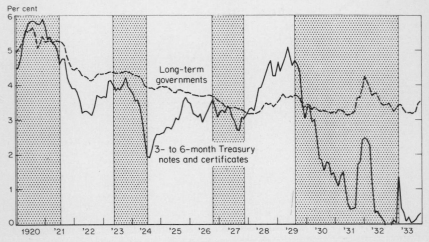

NOTE: Shaded areas represent business cycle contractions; unshaded areas,
expansions.

the 1920's are not directly comparable to those of the 1930's.
Despite these limitations, this body of data constitutes an important
and fruitful source of knowledge. It can reveal how the yields of
short- and long-term securities varied cyclically, and the extent to
which specific and reference cycles coincided.

Between 1920 and 1956, there were two subperiods when the rate
of interest for three- to six-month Treasury notes and certificates was
higher than the rate on long-term governments. These were from
June of 1920 through March of 1921, and from January 1928
through November 1929. For the balance of this period, short-term

government yields were always below long-term yields. The 1920–21 reversal of the usual relationship was both shorter and less pronounced than the later reversal. The maximum yield differential during the 1920–21 reversal was sixty-seven basis points; the average

CHART 8
Yields of U.S. Government Securities, 1934–41

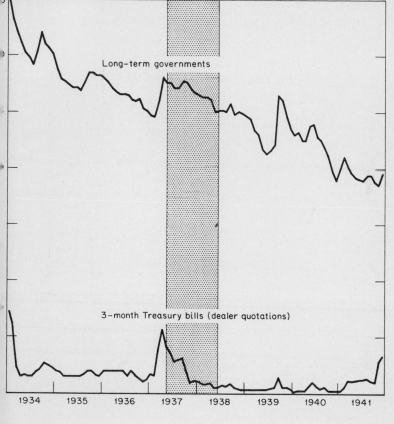

r cent

Long-term governments

3-month Treasury bills (dealer quotations)

1934   1935   1936   1937   1938   1939   1940   1941

NOTE: Shaded areas represent business cycle contractions; unshaded areas, expansions.

differential was thirty-three basis points. For the later period, 1928–29, the maximum differential was 145 basis points; the average was ninety-one. For nine months in 1957 and eight months in 1959 and 1960, nine- to twelve-month government yields were above the

TABLE 10

CYCLICAL CHANGES IN YIELDS OF GOVERNMENT SECURITIES,
1921-45

Business Cycles			Absolute Values			Changes	
Trough	Peak	Trough	Trough	Peak	Trough	Trough to Peak	Peak to Trough
A. Long-term governments[a]			5.26	4.37	3.94	-.89	-.43
July 1921-May 1923-July 1924			3.94	3.68	3.23	-.26	-.45
Nov. 1927-Aug.1929-Mar. 1933			3.23	3.71	3.42	.48	-.29
Mar. 1933-May 1937-June 1938			3.42	2.80	2.58	-.62	-.22
June 1938-Feb.1945-Oct. 1945			2.58	2.38	2.35	-.20	-.03
B. Short-term governments[b]							
July 1921-May 1923-July 1924			4.60	3.95	1.92	-.65	-2.03
July 1926-Oct.1926-Nov. 1927			1.92	3.58	3.04	1.66	-.54
Nov. 1927-Aug.1929-Mar. 1933			3.04	4.70	1.34	1.66	-3.36
Mar. 1933-May 1937-June 1938			2.29	.65	.02	-1.64	-.63
June 1938-Feb.1945-Oct. 1945			.05	.38	.38	.33	0

[a]First Three Cycles: Board of Governors of the Federal Reserve System, *Banking and Monetary Statistics*, Washington, D.C., 1943, Table 128, p. 468.
Last Two Cycles: Federal Reserve Board bill dealer quotations series (average yields on all outstanding fully taxable bonds due or callable after 12 years for March 1933 and after 15 years for May 1937, June 1938, Feb. 1945, and Oct. 1945).

[b]First Three Cycles: Three- to six-month Treasury notes and certificates, *Banking and Monetary Statistics*, Table 122, p. 460.
Fourth Cycle: Treasury bill new issues, *Banking and Monetary Statistics*, Table 122, p. 460.
Fifth Cycle: Three-month Treasury bill dealer quotations series from the *Federal Reserve Bulletin.*

TABLE 11

AVERAGE YIELD AND STANDARD DEVIATION IN YIELDS OF GOVERNMENT
SECURITIES DURING FIVE BUSINESS CYCLES,
1921-45

Business Cycle, Trough to Trough	Long-Term Governments		Short-Term Governments	
	Average Yield	Standard Deviation	Average Yield	Standard Deviation
June 1921-July 1924	4.39	.29	3.71	.56
July 1924-Nov. 1927	3.68	.23	3.04	.42
Nov. 1927-March 1933	3.44	.24	2.44	1.63
March 1933-June 1938	2.89	.26	.26	.32
June 1938-Oct. 1945	2.36	.18	.22	.16

Source: See Table 10.

twenty-year bond rate. The maximum differential in 1959–60 was twice that in 1957; seventy-eight basis points compared with thirty-eight (see Charts 6 and 7).

For the prewar cycles, the trough-to-peak and peak-to-trough movements in short-term rates were typically greater than the movements in long-term rates (see Table 10). In this respect, the cyclical behavior of interest rates before and after World War II are similar. Only for the wartime cycle, 1938–45, when the Treasury bill rate was constant for long periods as a result of the government support program, is the variation in the long-term rate greater than in the short-term rate. This seems to be directly attributable to the pegging of the rate on three-month bills by the government.

TABLE 12

TIMING OF SHORT- AND LONG-TERM YIELDS OF GOVERNMENT
SECURITIES AT BUSINESS CYCLE PEAKS AND TROUGHS,
1921–45

	Lead(−) or Lag(+) in Months, at Business Cycle Peaks and Troughs										
Government Securities	7/21 T	5/23 P	7/24 T	10/26 P	11/27 T	8/29 P	3/33 T	5/37 P	6/38 T	2/45 P	10/45 T
Short-term	+13	+5	+1	−11	−2	−3	−4	−1	+19	a	a
Long-term	+13	+5	a	a	+4	−5	+47	+5	+40	−7	+6

a No specific cycle.

For each of the five prewar cycles shown in Table 11, short-term government yields were, on average, below long-term yields (see Table 11). Hence, for each of the nine complete cycles in the 1921–61 period for which yields of long- and short-term governments are currently available, yield curves for governments probably had a positive slope, on the average. Similarly, the yield variance of short-term governments, with the exception of the wartime cycle, was greater than that of long-term governments.

The association of specific with business cycle turning points is stronger for the postwar cycles than for the five cycles from 1921 to 1945 (see Table 12). Between 1921 and 1945, unlike the later period, there are turning points of interest rate cycles whose association with business cycle peaks and troughs is tenuous at best. In the

CHART 9

*Average Pattern of Long-Term and Short-Term Interest Rates in the
United States During Fourteen Business Cycles, 1858–1914*

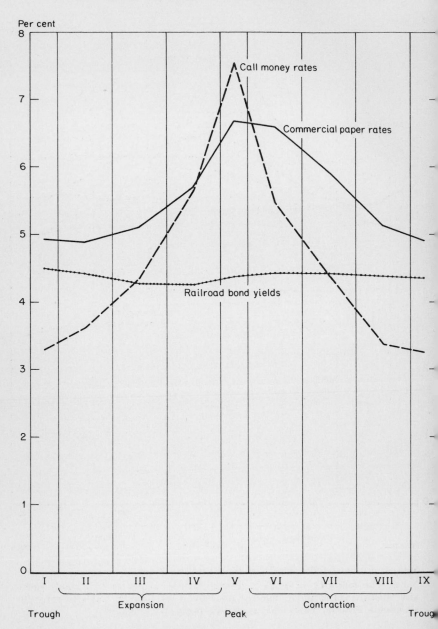

SOURCE: See notes following Chart 12.

CHART 10
Average Pattern of Long-Term and Short-Term Interest Rates in the United States During Five Business Cycles, 1914–33

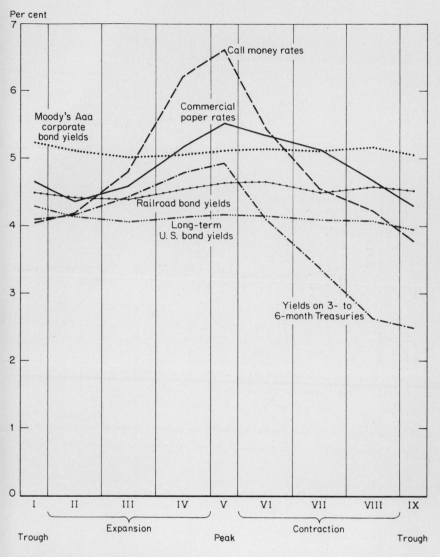

SOURCE: See notes following Chart 12.

NOTE: The following series cover shorter periods: long-term U.S. bonds yields and Moody's Aaa corporate bond yields, four cycles, 1919–33; yields on three- to six-month Treasury notes and certificates, three cycles, 1921–33.

1930's and early 1940's, specific cycles are less well defined than they were during either the 1920's or the post-World War II era. Nevertheless, the generalization that the gap between long- and short-term rates is small when rates are high and large when rates are low still seems to be supported by the data (see Charts 7 and 8).

Yields of nongovernmental obligations can provide insights into the cyclical behavior of interest rates before World War I. Since the issuers of long maturities are not the same as the issuers of short maturities, one hesitates to use these data for comparing the yields on different maturities. The series appear to be more useful for examining the cyclical changes in relative yields. Chart 9 summarizes these data from about the beginning of the Civil War until World War I. For the fourteen cycles in this period, short-term rates rose relative to long-term rates during expansions and fell during contractions. The peaks in the long-term rate occurred about midway in the business contraction, and the troughs occurred about midway in the expansion. The same data are carried forward from 1914 through 1933 in Chart 10. Again, short-term rates rose relative to long-term rates during expansions and fell during contractions. In this period, the peaks in the long-term rate more nearly matched business peaks, although troughs continued to occur after those in business. The same implications for the relative movements of long- and short-term rates during the business cycle may be drawn from these series for the 1945–61 period (see Chart 11). Only for 1933 through 1945, when the yields of governments also behaved anomalously, is the pattern—the relative rise of short-term rates during expansions and their fall during contractions—broken [4] (see Chart 12). This is a period when specific cycles conformed least with peaks and troughs in business conditions.

An independent body of data that reflects the term structure of interest rates from 1900 to date was initiated by Durand and sub-

[4] Hicks reports that short-term rates averaged less than long-term rates in England from 1850 through 1930. He uses risk premiums as the explanation for the observed yield differential. See John R. Hicks, "Mr. Hawtrey on Bank Rates and the Long Term Rate of Interest," *The Manchester School of Economic and Social Studies,* October 1939, p. 28.

Hawtrey reports that interest rates have varied cyclically in England, with short-term rates relatively low during depressions and high during booms. See Ralph G. Hawtrey, *A Century of Bank Rates,* London, 1938, pp. 167 ff.

CHART 11

Average Pattern of Long-Term and Short-Term Interest Rates in the United States During Four Business Cycles, 1945–61

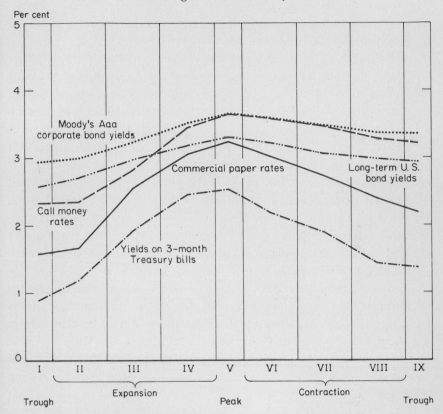

SOURCE: See notes following Chart 12.

CHART 12

Average Pattern of Long-Term and Short-Term Interest Rates in the
United States During Two Business Cycles, 1933–45

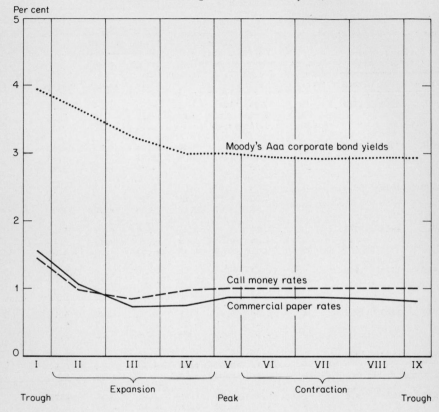

SOURCE TO CHARTS 9 THROUGH 12

Call money rates
  1858–1936: Frederick R. Macaulay, Some Theoretical Problems Suggested by
  the Movements of Interest Rates, Bond Yields and Stock Prices in the United
  States since 1856, New York, NBER, 1938, Appendix A.
  1937–61: Survey of Current Business, U.S. Department of Commerce.
Commercial paper rates
  1858–Jan. 1937: Macaulay, Movements of Interest Rates.
  Feb. 1937–61: Compiled by NBER from weekly rates in Bank and Quotation
  Record, William B. Dana Co.
Railroad bond yields
  Macaulay, Movements of Interest Rates. The series used is adjusted for "eco-
  nomic drift."
Moody's Aaa, corporate bond yields
  Moody's Industrial Manual, Moody's Investors' Service
Long-term U.S. bond yields
  Federal Reserve Bulletin, Board of Governors of the Federal Reserve System

TABLE 13

BASIC YIELDS ON CORPORATE BONDS DURING BUSINESS CYCLES,
1900–61
(per cent)

Business Cycle (fiscal years)			Term to Maturity (years)	Yield at Business Cycle			Change in Yield		
Trough	Peak	Trough		Trough (T)	Peak (P)	Trough (T)	Trough to Peak	Peak to Trough	Cycle Average [a]
1901	1903	1904	1	3.25	3.45	3.60	+.20	+.15	3.39
			5	3.25	3.45	3.60	+.20	+.15	3.39
			20	3.25	3.45	3.60	+.20	+.15	3.39
1904	1907	1908	1	3.60	4.87	5.10	+1.27	+.23	4.37
			5	3.60	3.87	4.30	+.27	+.43	3.75
			20	3.60	3.80	3.95	+.20	+.15	3.66
1908	1910	1911	1	5.10	4.25	4.09	−.85	−.16	4.29
			5	4.30	4.10	4.05	−.20	−.05	4.08
			20	3.95	3.87	3.94	−.08	+.07	3.88
1911	1913	1915	1	4.09	4.74	4.47	+.65	−.27	4.42
			5	4.05	4.31	4.39	+.26	+.08	4.24
			20	3.94	4.02	4.20	+.08	+.18	4.04
1915	1918	1919	1	4.47	5.48	5.58	+1.01	+.10	4.51
			5	4.39	5.25	5.16	+.86	−.09	4.53
			20	4.20	4.82	4.81	+.62	−.01	4.36
1919	1920	1922	1	5.58	6.11	5.31	+.53	−.80	6.16
			5	5.16	5.72	5.19	+.56	−.53	5.70
			20	4.81	5.17	4.85	+.36	−.32	5.10
1922	1923	1924	1	5.31	5.01	5.02	−.30	+.01	5.09
			5	5.19	4.90	4.90	−.29	0	4.97
			20	4.85	4.68	4.69	−.17	+.01	4.72
1924	1927	1928	1	5.02	4.30	4.05	−.72	−.25	4.27
			5	4.90	4.30	4.05	−.60	−.25	4.41
			20	4.69	4.30	4.05	−.39	−.25	4.39
1928	1929	1933	1	4.05	5.27	2.60	+1.22	−2.67	4.01
			5	4.05	4.72	3.68	+.67	−1.04	4.29
			20	4.05	4.45	4.11	+.40	−.34	4.35
1933	1937	1939	1	2.60	.69	.57	−1.91	−.12	1.23
			5	3.68	1.68	1.55	−2.00	−.13	2.33
			20	4.11	2.90	2.65	−1.21	−.25	3.25
1939	1945	1946	1	.57	1.02	.86	+.45	−.16	0.80
			5	1.55	1.53	1.32	−.02	−.21	1.46
			20	2.65	2.55	2.35	−.10	−.20	2.56

(continued)

TABLE 13 (concluded)

Business Cycle (fiscal years)			Term to Maturity (years)	Yield at Business Cycle			Change in Yield		
Trough	Peak	Trough		Trough (T)	Peak (P)	Trough (T)	Trough to Peak	Peak to Trough	Cycle Average[a]
1946	1948	1950	1	.86	1.60	1.42	+.74	-.18	1.35
			5	1.32	2.03	1.90	+.71	-.13	1.80
			20	2.35	2.73	2.48	+.38	-.25	2.54
1950	1953	1954	1	1.42	2.62	2.40	+1.20	-.22	2.33
			5	1.90	2.75	2.52	+.85	-.23	2.48
			20	2.48	3.05	2.88	+.57	-.17	2.80
1954	1957	1958	1	2.40	3.50	3.21	+1.10	-.29	2.90
			5	2.52	3.50	3.25	+.98	-.25	2.97
			20	2.88	3.50	3.47	+.62	-.03	3.15
1958	1960	1961	1	3.21	4.95	3.10	+1.74	-1.85	3.92
			5	3.25	4.73	3.75	+1.48	-.98	4.01
			20	3.47	4.55	4.12	+1.08	-.43	4.15

Source: 1900–42, David Durand, *Basic Yields of Corporate Bonds, 1900–1942* New York, NBER, Technical Paper 3, 1942, pp. 5–6.

1943–47, David Durand and Willis J. Winn, *Basic Yields of Bonds, 1926–1947: Their Measurement and Pattern,* New York, NBER, Technical Paper 6, 1947, p. 14.

1948–61, National Industrial Conference Board, *The Economic Almanac 1962,* p. 353.

The business cycle peak and trough dates are from the National Bureau's fiscal year chronology. The basic yields are available only for the first quarter of each calendar year; the yield for the first quarter of 1901 is entered in the fiscal year ended June 30, 1901, etc.

[a]The initial and terminal trough years each receive a weight of 1/2; the intervening years, a weight of 1.

sequently maintained by other observers. These data show yields as of the first quarter of every year for high-grade or default-free corporate bonds as a function of term to maturity. They were assembled by plotting yields of high-grade corporate bonds, fitting curves to the lower bounds of these data, and subsequently observing the points on these yield curves that correspond to particular terms to maturity. These data are summarized in Table 13 and Chart 13.

Durand's observations suggest that the swings in short-term rates are typically greater than the swings in long-term rates. When rates conformed to the business cycle, the term structure was less steeply inclined at peaks and troughs. During the early part of this period, conformity with the cycle was poorer than in the later part.

Durand's observations are consistent with the time series already

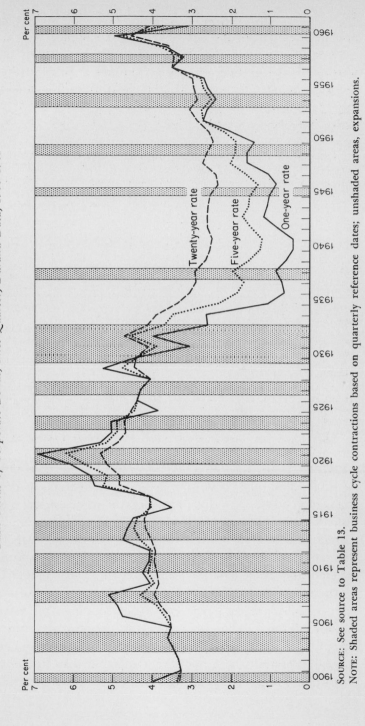

CHART 13

Basic Yields of Corporate Bonds, First Quarter, Durand Data, 1900–1961

SOURCE: See source to Table 13.

NOTE: Shaded areas represent business cycle contractions based on quarterly reference dates; unshaded areas, expansions.

presented, except for the 1920's. During this decade, time series for governments indicate that the average yields of short maturities were below that of long maturities. Durand's findings indicate just the opposite. Durand recognizes the existence of this inconsistency; indeed, for the same year he reports yield curves with opposite slopes but offers no explanation.[5]

[5] Two possible lines of explanation, other than errors of observation, come to mind. (1) At this time, long governments were partially tax exempt, short governments totally tax exempt. (2) Transactions costs for short, relative to long, governments are lower than they are for short, relative to long, corporates.

4

THE APPLICATION OF
THE LIQUIDITY PREFERENCE
AND EXPECTATIONS HYPOTHESES
TO THE CYCLICAL BEHAVIOR
OF INTEREST RATES

A. Applications of the Lutz-Meiselman Model

IF BOTH liquidity effects and incorrect expectations are disregarded, one should expect to find that long-term rates are higher than short-term rates when the latter are low and lower than short-term rates when the latter are high; in the absence of trends in interest rates, the average yields of short- and long-term rates should be equal. Insofar as short-term rates are relatively low about cyclical troughs and high about peaks, yield curves ought to be negatively sloped at peaks and positively sloped at troughs. Peaks and troughs in specific cycles of short-term rates should be anticipated by movements in long-term rates. If the market anticipates increases or decreases in short-term rates, long-term rates should move in advance in the same direction. Hence, if peaks and troughs in short-term rates are coincident with the reference cycle, peaks and troughs in long-term rates ought to lead the business cycle, and the longer the maturity, the greater the lead. The reasoning here is the same as that which led Macaulay to expect time money rates to lead call money rates.

Analytically, the 91-day bill rate can be regarded as a spot or instantaneous rate of interest which reflects money market conditions at specific phases of the cycle. In contrast, the yield on long-term governments represents an average of the current and expected spot rates over the course of three or four reference cycles. Because the term to maturity of long-term governments is longer than the usual reference cycle, the yields of these securities reflect an average of spot rates during both expansions and contractions. Hence, long-term rates vary relatively less than short-term rates. Money market conditions during a specific phase of a cycle are largely "averaged out" (the effects of abnormally low or high spot rates largely cancel) in the determination of the long-term rate. In contrast, money market conditions during specific cycle phases are completely reflected in bill yields. As a result, short-term rates ought to be more variable over the cycle than long-term rates. The expectations hypothesis implies that the shorter the term to maturity of a security, the smaller the number of spot rates that are averaged in order to determine its yield; consequently, the larger its variance over the cycle. Cyclical movements in the short- relative to the long-term rate can be analyzed as if the latter were a permanent or normal rate of interest and the short-term rate contained a large transitory component. This transitory component is largest about peaks and troughs. When positive, at peaks, short-term rates are high relative to long-term rates; when negative, at troughs, short-term rates are relatively low.[1]

The market regards current short-term rates as abnormally high when they are above long-term rates, and expects them to fall in the future. At such times, holders of long-term securities expect

---

[1] This implies that the correlation between a moving average of short-term rates and long-term rates over the cycle would be greater than the correlation between current short- with long-term rates. A moving average would abstract from cyclical effects on short-term rates; it would depict permanent short-term rates and abstract from transitory effects. It also would, of course, reduce the amplitude of the fluctuations in short- relative to long-term rates; in effect, it converts short- to long-term rates.

The view that the long-term rate is an average of short-term rates explains why Hicks found that time series of short- and long-term rates were less strongly correlated than averages of past and present short-term rates (both weighted and unweighted) and long-term rates. Presumably averages reflect expectations of "permanent" short-term rates. Hence they are more like long-term rates than actual short-term rates which embody a transitory component that is negative at troughs and positive at peaks. See Hicks, "Mr. Hawtrey On Bank Rates," p. 28. Hawtrey's position is similar to that of Charles C. Abbott, "A Note on the Government Bond Market," *The Review of Economic Statistics*, Vol. 17, 1935, p. 9. Both reasoned that the forces that affect short maturity yields are largely independent of the forces that affect long maturity yields because fluctuations in short-term rates are much greater than those in long-term rates.

to win capital gains because the passage of time will eliminate the abnormally high short-term rates from the average of present and future short-term rates that is the long-term rate. The opposite occurs when short-term rates are relatively low; i.e., the holders of long-term securities expect to incur capital losses as low short-term rates are eliminated from the average that is the long-term rate.

This does not, in itself, imply that it is more profitable to hold long- than short-term securities when rates are expected to fall. If the expectations of the market are correct, then the high yields of short- relative to long-term securities would just offset expected capital gains on the latter. The yield differential in this case represents what the market thinks is necessary to equalize the holding period yields of these securities, taking into account both coupons and capital gains. Conversely, when short-term rates are abnormally low, they are expected to rise. The abnormally large yield advantage of long-term securities in this case represents what the market thinks is necessary to offset the expected capital losses attributable to holding them. Whether or not the holding period yields of short-term relative to long-term securities are greater or less over the cycle depends upon which way the market erred in predicting future short-term rates. A fall in short-term rates that is larger than anticipated favors the holders of long-term securities, and vice versa.

These implications of the expectations hypothesis for the cyclical behavior of interest rates are in part incorrect because liquidity preference is not an independent variable in the analysis. Yet they go far towards providing an interpretation of the behavior of yield differentials between long- and short-term governments since 1920. In particular, they further our understanding of the sharp movements in short-term rates that occurred during this time.

In the 1920's there were two periods when short-term rates were above long-term rates (see Chart 7). During 1920, and again in 1929, the market anticipated lower future short-term rates. Although the absolute level of short-term rates during 1920 was about seventy-five basis points higher than it was in 1929, the anticipated fall was much greater in 1929. The yield advantage of short-term over long-term securities in 1929 was at least twice as great as it was in 1921. The fall in short-term rates from 1929 to 1931 was about 450 basis points, whereas the fall from 1920 to 1922 was about 275 basis points. Both downward movements were greater than the other declines in short-term rates during this period.

In more recent years (1957 and 1959), short-term rates were again higher than long-term rates (see Chart 6). The absolute level of rates was higher in 1959 but the yield differential between long- and short-term securities was about the same. The subsequent downward movements in short-term rates were of roughly equal magnitude, about 275 basis points, and were the largest declines since the 1920's. In the 1930's, short-term relative to long-term rates were especially low. This was a consequence of abnormally low short-term rates; they were at historical lows.

The implications of a pure expectations model for the cyclical behavior of interest rates are inconsistent with the following observations: (1) short maturities yield less over the cycle than long maturities; yield curves are more often than not positively sloped; (2) short-term rates fail to exceed long-term rates at peaks as much as they fall below long-term rates at troughs; (3) the variance over the cycle in yields of three-month Treasury bills is less than the variance of nine- to twelve-month governments; (4) when short-term rates are above long-term rates, it is not the shortest term to maturity that bears the highest yield, i.e., yield curves at first rise with term to maturity and then fall; (5) long-term rates fail to lead turning points in short-term rates.

B. Applications of the Hicks Model

1. CYCLICAL BEHAVIOR OF GOVERNMENTS

To explain these observations, liquidity preference must be added to the analysis. This implies that interest rates no longer measure the total return derived from holding securities. Securities also yield a nonpecuniary or liquidity income to their holders. The evidence presented indicates that the nonpecuniary return from securities is inversely related to term to maturity and directly related to the level of pecuniary yields. The shorter the term to maturity, the larger the fraction of the total return from a security that is nonpecuniary, and vice versa. The higher the level of interest rates, the wider the spread between the total return from a security and its pecuniary yield, and vice versa.

If, abstracting from differences in expectations of future short-term rates, the total return attributable to all maturities is the same, i.e., the sum of pecuniary and nonpecuniary returns is equal for all terms to maturity, then the pecuniary yield must be an increasing function of term to maturity. Therefore, if expectations have a

CHART 14

"Normal" or Average Yield Curve

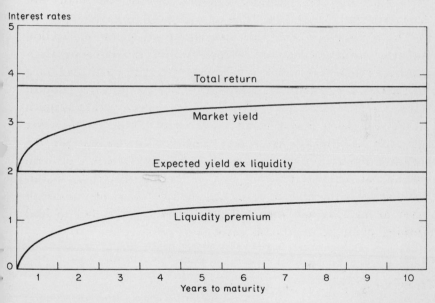

random effect on yield curves, the average yield curve will be positively sloped, and short-term rates will, on the average, be lower than long-term rates. The interaction of expectations and liquidity preference to produce a "normal" yield curve is shown in Chart 14. The "total return" curve is flat; it depicts a market in which future short-term rates are expected to be the same as the current rates. The liquidity yield is the fraction of total yields for any given maturity that is nonpecuniary. Subtracting the nonpecuniary component from total return leaves the pecuniary yield curve, which is the yield curve observed in the market.[2]

Liquidity preference produces asymmetry in the relationship between short- and long-term rates at cycle peaks and troughs. It accounts for the failure of short-term rates to exceed long-term rates at peaks by as much as they fall below long-term rates at troughs.

CHART 15
Yield Curve at Cyclical Troughs

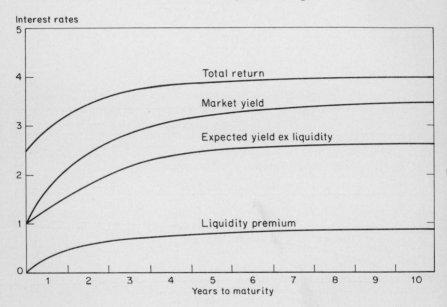

At cyclical troughs, both liquidity and expectational forces operate independently to establish short-term rates below long-term rates. Liquidity preference produces a pecuniary yield differential of long-term over short-term securities. At troughs, the market regards the current short-term rate as abnormally low and expects it to be

[2] Liquidity return as a percentage of total return was obtained by first fitting a yield curve to average yields as a function of term to maturity for the three latest reference cycles. Then the ratios of yields for particular maturities to twenty-year government bond yields were computed. The difference between the ratio for any given term to maturity and one constitutes the fraction of total yield that is nonpecuniary for that term to maturity.

higher in the future. Hence, expectations also push short-term below long-term rates. Both effects operate to widen the spread between these rates (Chart 15). The total-return curve slopes positively because the market expects future yields on short maturities, both pecuniary and nonpecuniary, to be higher than current short maturity yields. Subtracting the liquidity component from the total yield curve produces a market yield curve with a long-short differ-

CHART 16
A Flat Yield Curve

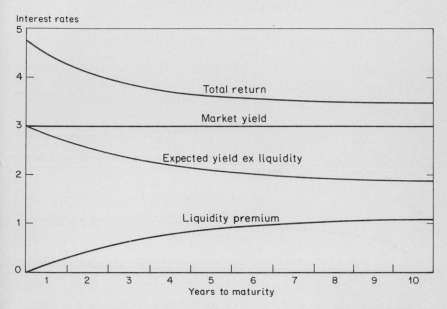

ential greater than the differential for the corresponding total yield curve.

At cyclical peaks, in contrast to cyclical troughs, liquidity and expectational forces produce opposite effects on yield curves. Liquidity preference, as always, operates to establish short-term below long-term rates. However, expectations act in the opposite direction. Because the market expects future short-term rates to be lower, the total yield curve declines as a function of term to maturity. Whether or not the resulting market yield curve is rising, falling, or both depends upon the relative strength of these opposing forces. Because these forces work in opposite directions at cyclical peaks but in the same direction at troughs, short-term yields do not exceed long-term yields at peaks as much as they fall below long-term yields at troughs.

The foregoing analysis implies that flat market yield curves should be interpreted as indicating that the market expects future pecuniary yields of short maturities to be lower than current short-term rates. With no change in expectations, the fraction of the total

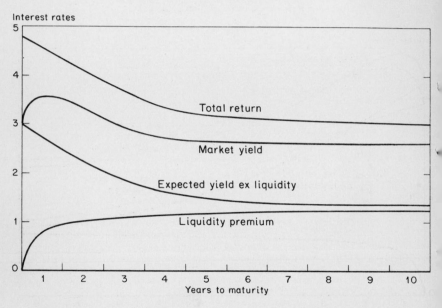

CHART 17

Yield Curve at Cyclical Peaks

return that is nonpecuniary for a forward rate which pertains to a specific period of calendar time will rise with the passage of time. Hence, its pecuniary yield will fall below current spot rates. A flat market yield curve is shown in Chart 16. A falling total-return curve is a necessary condition for its existence.

Charts 17 and 18 depict yield curves with segments that are negatively sloped (yield curves with such shapes are also referred to as humped). Such curves are produced by expectations of sharply falling interest rates, i.e., interest rates that are falling more sharply than those in Chart 15. The more sharply interest rates are expected to fall, the shorter the term to maturity of the peak in yields; the more gradual the expected fall, the further out on the yield curve the peak will be. If the expected fall in short-term rates is very gradual, no negative segment appears. Yield curves with negative segments have been relatively rare, at least since the 1920's; expectations of interest-rate declines are usually not sharp enough to offset the effects of liquidity preference.

CHART 18

Effects of Alternative Expectations of Falling Rates upon the Shapes of Yield Curves

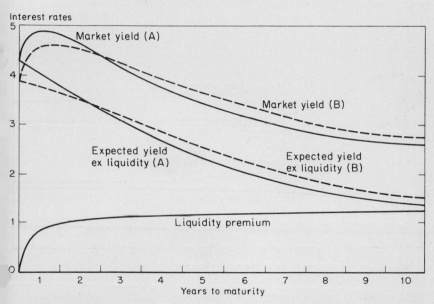

Liquidity preference also explains why the shortest term to maturity is not the highest yielding security in the term structure at cyclical peaks. In order for a yield curve to exist that has the shortest term to maturity bearing the highest yield, expectations of extremely sharp declines in short-term rates are required. Such expectations, while a theoretical possibility, did not exist during the two most recent cyclical peaks and possibly have never existed.

The liquidity preference hypothesis implies that nonpecuniary yields are a decreasing function of term to maturity. Hence, the range of pecuniary yields that will be observed in the market will increase with term to maturity. For example, suppose liquidity yields for Treasury bills and nine- to twelve-month governments are at all times 50 and 25 per cent of total returns. Further, assume that total returns, which are of course not directly observable in the market, range from 4 to 8 per cent. Pecuniary yields will then range from 2 to 4 per cent for bills, and from 3 to 6 per cent for nine- to twelve-month governments. Hence liquidity preference implies that the variance in yields over the cycle increases with term to maturity.

The expectations hypothesis implies just the opposite: that the shorter the term to maturity, the greater the variance. Therefore, the actual variance observed in the market for any specified term to maturity represents a composition of these conflicting forces. The available evidence on variance as a function of term to maturity suggests that liquidity effects dominate expectational effects for governments with maturities equal to or less than nine-to-twelve months. For three- to five-year governments and longer maturities, expectational effects dominate. The absence of time series between these maturity ranges precludes a precise estimate here of the borderline separating the domains of dominance of expectations and liquidity.

During expansions, yield differentials between Treasury bills and nine- to twelve-month governments widen. Insofar as liquidity effects dominate expectational effects, liquidity premiums ought to widen from trough to peak since, according to the liquidity preference hypothesis, they are an increasing function of the absolute level of interest rates. Consequently, if only liquidity effects are at work, the differentials between bills and nine- to twelve-month governments would increase more than the increases observed. Adding expectations to the analysis implies, given the assumption that the market can recognize transitorily high or low levels of spot rates, the addition of an opposing force. Converse implications are implied for contractions. Liquidity operates to narrow, and expectations to widen, the spread between bills and nine- to twelve-month governments. Since liquidity is dominant for this maturity range, the observed spreads decrease during contractions. For evidence on how these differentials have actually behaved, see Charts 5 and 6.

These findings for governments do not necessarily apply to corporates or to the issues of government agencies unless the nonpecuniary component of total yield is the same. In general, governments appear to be more liquid, ignoring the influence of term to maturity, than either agency issues or corporates.[3] Among short-term securities, governments have a comparative liquidity advantage over agencies or corporates. The bill market has very low transactions costs and bid and asked prices are firm for extremely large transactions. This suggests that when yield curves are humped, the peak in yields will have a longer term to maturity for corporates than for governments.

In the absence of liquidity premiums, and assuming the market can forecast turning points in the specific cycles of interest rates, cyclical peaks in long-term rates would precede those of short-term rates and would be observable first. Similarly, troughs in long-term rates would precede troughs in short-term rates. The rationale that Macaulay used to argue that the seasonal peak in time money rates should precede that in call money rates is relevant here. Insofar as the market can predict turning points in short-term rates, the long-term rate (which is an average of future short-term rates) should reach its peak first in anticipation of the peak in short-term rates.

When liquidity preference is introduced into the analysis, however, the sequence in the timing of peaks and troughs of long- and short-term securities becomes less obvious. If liquidity premiums are a function of spot rates, then an amount is added to long-term rates which increases as short-term rates increase and reaches a peak when the latter reach their peak. The peak in long-term rates must

---

[3] The evidence for the proposition that agency issues are less liquid than governments is of two kinds. (1) Agencies have higher transactions costs. The spread between bid and asked prices, as reported in dealer quotation sheets, ranges from two-thirty-seconds for short-term securities to a whole point, the equivalent of ten dollars, for long-term securities. (2) The value of agencies as collateral for bank loans is poorer than it is for governments. Per dollar of borrowing, the market value of collateral in the form of agencies, term to maturity aside, is higher than it is for governments. The Joint Economic Committee *Study of the Dealer Market*, p. 95, reports that the margin requirements for agencies are 5 per cent.

occur later, therefore, than it would have occurred in a world of pure expectations.

How much later this peak will occur can only be partially determined by a priori reasoning. It is clear that the peak in long-term rates should not occur after the peak in short-term rates. Since the maximum amount that will be added to long-term rates because of liquidity preference will occur when short-term rates reach their peak, the peak in long-term rates must either precede or be synchronous with that of short-term rates.

Since the end of World War II, the behavior of time series of governments with various terms to maturity indicates that all securities, irrespective of maturity, reach their peaks and troughs synchronously. Hence, without going further into the question of whether liquidity premiums add enough to long-term rates to delay their peaks until all peaks are synchronous, irrespective of term to maturity, one cannot say, using this evidence alone, whether the market can or cannot predict turning points in interest rates. In view of the inability of the market to predict turning points of other series, on balance, it seems reasonable to interpret these findings as being consistent with the view that the market cannot predict turning points in specific cycles of interest rates.[4]

2. CYCLICAL BEHAVIOR OF AGENCY ISSUES AND CORPORATES

The thesis has been advanced that liquidity premiums are caused primarily by a desire to avoid the risk of capital loss. The evidence indicates that yield differentials, when only liquidity differences exist, increase with the absolute level of rates. The observations of an upward trend in liquidity premiums for the three latest cycles, and regressions of liquidity premiums upon spot rates, show that liquidity premiums increase when interest rates increase. This thesis has implications for the cyclical and secular behavior of other rates of interest. It implies that low-quality bonds ought to yield

---

4 The highest correlation (.98) of seasonally adjusted time series for three-month Treasury bills with nine- to twelve-month governments was obtained by assuming the two series to be synchronous. The correlations with one-, two-, and three-month leads and lags were: .95 for one month, .90 for two, and .83 for three. No difference, to two decimal places, was observed for leads and lags of equal duration.

more, the cycle aside, than high-quality bonds because they are relatively less liquid, i.e., price variance is greater as a result of the greater default risk. Consequently, it should be possible to observe that high-quality bonds yield less than low-quality bonds generally and that the yield differential between high- and low-quality bonds increases from trough to peak, and decreases from peak to trough. By symmetrical reasoning, the spread between government agency issues and governments, ignoring term to maturity, should increase with the absolute level of interest rates.

To test one of these propositions, yield differentials between governments and government agency issues were regressed against their sums. The results of this test are mixed. For nine- to twelve-month maturities, the spreads between governments on the one hand, and Federal National Mortgage Association, Federal Land Bank, and Federal Home Loan Bank issues on the other, are consistent with the hypothesis advanced; spreads increase as the absolute level of interest rates increase. The same is true for maturities ten years and over. The best results were obtained by regressing the yield differential between a government bond, the three and one-quarter of 1983, and an index of AA utility yields of bonds with coupons of three and one-eighth to three and three-eighths against their sum. The correlation was positive and 40 per cent of the variation in the spread was explained.[5] However, for three- to five-year governments and FLB and FNMA issues, the slopes of the regression coefficients were negative, one significantly so.

The consequences of changes in the level of interest rates for yield differentials between low- and high-quality bonds over the cycle is somewhat more difficult to detect. During contractions, the level of rates falls and the market usually increases its estimates of the risks of default by the issuers of low-quality securities. Conversely, the level of rates rises during expansions and the market usually decreases its estimates of the risks of default. Hence, li-

---

[5] All of the agency issues exhibited a significant downward trend over time in yield differentials compared with governments. Presumably this reflects the diffusion of knowledge about the investment merits of these securities that has occurred in recent years. The data for the agencies consist of incomplete series, mostly for the last decade, compiled by Charles E. Quincey and Co., and Allen Knowles, the fiscal agent of the Federal Home Loan Banks. The AA utility series is compiled by Salomon Bros. & Hutzler.

quidity and cyclical forces work in opposite directions upon yield differentials. During the post-World War II period, the revaluation of risks over the cycle has dominated liquidity forces. Hence, the yields of Baa Moody's bonds, for all categories, have fluctuated less than corresponding Aaa bonds.

The behavior of low- and high-quality bond yield differentials over time seems to support the view that the level of rates and these differentials are related. Since 1945, the spread between Moody's AAA and BAA series has increased with the level of interest rates. The regression of the difference on the sum indicates that the difference rises with the level of rates.

Prewar investigations of the relationship between the yield differential of high- and low-grade bonds and the level of interest rates also conforms to this finding.

Ratios of promised yields (or yield spreads) to the basic rates on high-grade issues deserve more attention than they can be given in this report. According to the classical theory of investment values, the simple yield spread, or algebraic difference between the promised yield and basic rate, would provide the best measure of the risk premium for issues properly priced in the market, since the yield is conceived of as the algebraic sum of the pure rate of interest and the risk premium. It is a matter of record, however, that yield spreads frequently narrow when basic rates fall, and widen when basic rates rise . . . , perhaps because of the efforts of investors to compensate for changes in basic rates.[6]

For any preassigned cyclical downturn in bill rates, yield differentials between low- and high-grade bonds should decrease most during severe and least during mild contractions. Conversely, during strong upturns, the differential ought to increase more for sharp than for mild recoveries. The data on the behavior of differentials between low- and high-grade bonds, since the end of World War II, while they support the view that there has been a secular rise in the differential, do not support the view that the differential is at a maximum at peaks and minimum at troughs. In fact, the maximum differential seems to appear midway between the cyclical peak and the trough. This seems to be accounted for by differences

[6] W. Braddock Hickman, *Corporate Bond Quality and Investor Experience*, Princeton University Press for National Bureau of Economic Research, 1958, p. 288. For further discussion, see following pages.

between low- and high-grade bonds in the timing of their specific cycle peaks and troughs. In the postwar period, specific cycle peaks and troughs of high-grade bonds consistently preceded those of low-grade bonds. Hence, the maximum yield differential between the two could not have been associated with business cycle turning points.[7]

Hickman's investigation of the relationship between low- and high-grade bond yields over time suggests that the long-run rate of return to investors in low-grade bonds is greater than it is for high-grade bonds. He concludes that "the highest returns were obtained by investors who could afford to take the greatest risks." [8] He found that both the variance and the average rate of return was greatest for investments in low-grade bonds. In this respect, his finding is symmetrical with the relationship between long- and short-term government yields, taking into account both capital gains and interest receipts.

---

[7] Part of the increase in the measured yield differential between low- and high-grade bonds is attributable to differences between the economic, as distinguished from the temporal, term to maturity of these bonds. If calendar term to maturity is the same for both grades, then economic term to maturity, which Macaulay termed duration, must be shorter on the lower-grade issues. (See *Movements of Interest Rates,* Chapter II, for a discussion of this point.) The weights assigned to receipts in the near, relative to the distant, future for computing yield to maturity is greater for low- than high-quality bonds. Hence, a rise in rates during an expansion, with no change in investor attitudes towards risk, will increase measured yield differentials for the same reason that yields of three- to five-year governments rise relative to twenty-year governments during an expansion. This same point explains why the market believes that if interest rates are expected to fall, securities with equal yields and terms to maturity will have different relative price rises if their coupons are not the same. The size of the coupons will be inversely related to the rate of change of capital values.

In fact, this phenomenon seems to account for a trivial portion of the cyclical variation in the yield differential between low- and high-quality bonds. To determine the quantitative importance of this effect, a constant risk differential of 1 per cent for all spot and forward rates was assumed for two hypothetical ten-year bonds. At peaks, the higher-grade bond was assumed to consist of a six-month spot rate of 5 per cent, with the first forward rate being 4.5 per cent and all succeeding forward rates, 4 per cent. At troughs, the higher-grade bond was assumed to consist of a six-month spot rate of 2 per cent, with the first forward rate being 3 per cent and all succeeding forward rates 4 per cent. The yield to maturity of these two postulated securities differed by ninety-eight basis points at troughs, and one hundred and two at peaks.

[8] Hickman, *Corporate Bond Quality,* p. 138.

5

CONCLUSIONS AND IMPLICATIONS
FOR FURTHER RESEARCH

THIS INVESTIGATION confirms the principal finding of Meiselman—
that a relationship exists between expectations of future short-term
rates and the term structure of interest rates. The fact that forward
rates incorporate predictions of future short-term rates, with an
appreciable accuracy in a statistical sense, demonstrates, by an a
fortiori argument, that forward rates are a function of expected
future spot rates.

Previous investigators, Hickman and Meiselman, have interpreted
the difference between forward and subsequently observed spot
rates as forecasting errors of the market. (Culbertson found the difference between holding period yields of different terms to maturity
to be so large that he rejected the view that the market forecasts,
since he found it difficult to believe that the market could forecast
as badly as his interpretation of his findings suggests.) Their interpretations can be questioned because it is unreasonable to expect
the market to err asymmetrically. The mean error in a long series of
observations should be zero. If the work of these investigators is ex-
tended or examined closely, it can be shown that what they regarded as forecasting errors were in large part attributable to liquidity premiums, and that the errors of the market were indeed much
smaller.

It is the thesis of this study that a forward rate should be viewed,
not as an expected rate, but as an expected rate plus a liquidity
premium. If forward rates are so interpreted, then the forecasts and
forecasting errors of the market can be detected. These forecasts
are, within the maturity spectrum studied, accurate to a degree
that cannot be rationalized as the workings of chance. The finding
that forward rates constitute high estimates of future spot rates is

consistent with the Keynesian theory of "normal backwardation." The implications of this theory for the money and capital markets have been developed by Hicks in *Value and Capital*.[1] Hence these results support the Hicksian view that forward rates are equal to expected spot rates plus a liquidity premium.

The existence of liquidity premiums indicates that short and long maturities are not perfect substitutes for one another in the market as the proponents of the pure expectations hypothesis, such as Lutz and Meiselman, have argued. In particular, short and long maturities differ with respect to their value as money substitutes; short maturities are much better money substitutes than long maturities. Consequently, the greater liquidity yield of short maturities leads to a persistent pecuniary yield differential in favor of long maturities. This differential offsets the greater liquidity yield of short maturities. Therefore, the expected value of holding period yields, (with yield defined as total, as distinguished from pecuniary only), is equal for all terms to maturity.

The existence of liquidity premiums has been explained as a consequence of risk avoidance and positive costs for the speculative services required to convert long- into short-term securities. The market is willing to take a lower yield in exchange for a lower variance in the price of governments. The implications of this rationalization are consistent with the observed behavior of relative yields of low- and high-grade bonds, both secularly and cyclically.

Liquidity premiums have moved with the cycle in recent years. Since interest rates also increase during expansions and decrease during contractions, this raises the question: are liquidity premiums a function of the stage of the cycle or the level of interest rates? The upward trend in liquidity premiums over the three latest cycles, when interest rates have also shown an upward trend, indicates that it is the level of interest rates and not the stage of the cycle that determines the magnitude of liquidity premiums.

This finding does not support the theory that liquidity premiums are a development of the Great Depression. It is difficult to understand why evidence of the existence of liquidity premiums was so sparse before the 1930's and so abundant afterwards. If one argues

[1] In particular, see p. 147.

that the emergence of liquidity premiums was a consequence of risk
aversion caused by the financial losses of the early 1930's, then one
ought to observe that liquidity premiums have been declining
secularly since that time. The foregoing evidence does not support
this view. However, possibly more refined analysis, when the level
of rates is held constant, would show that there has been a downward trend in liquidity premiums over time.

The joining of liquidity preference to expectations explains the
lack of symmetry in the movement of short- and long-term rates
over the cycle. It explains why short-term rates do not exceed long-
term rates at peaks by as much as they fall below long-term rates
at troughs; why yield curves are positively sloped during most of
the cycle; and why yield curves, when short-term rates are unusually
high, never seem to be negatively sloped throughout their full
length, but show humps near the short end.

The common belief that short-term rates fluctuate more than
long-term rates is, in general, correct.[2] However, this generalization
conceals an important observation—as term to maturity increases,
yield variance first increases, and then decreases. This observation
is inconsistent with a pure expectations hypothesis, but is consistent
with a hypothesis that combines expectations and liquidity forces.

At any instant of time, the power of the market to predict future
spot rates decreases the longer the time span between the moment
a forward rate is inferred from the term structure of interest rates
and the corresponding spot rate is observed. Clearly it is more
difficult to see one year than one week into the future. Hence, as
the span of time between the moment a forward rate is inferred and
the relevant spot rate is observed increases, the correlations between
forward and spot rates ought to decrease. The observations for
three- and six-month bills and one- and two-year governments are
consistent with this implication of the expectations hypothesis.
Other tests for this same period of time, but for different time
spans, between forward and spot rates ought to yield results consistent with the foregoing. Indeed, this argument implies that a

---

[2] This is only arithmetic in a world of perfect certainty. Long-term rates can
fluctuate more than short-term rates. The fact that they do not fluctuate as
much as short-term rates implies that the market has some powers to recognize
when short-term rates are transitorily high or low.

correlation between forward and two-year spot rates that is greater than the correlation between forward and one-year spot rates would contradict the expectations hypothesis.

The data used to show that the expectations hypothesis has predictive content is primarily drawn from one business cycle, 1958–61. Possibly using this particular cycle has produced freakish results and comparable findings could not be obtained for other cycles. Clearly much more work can and should be undertaken to find out just how well the market can predict. In particular, an effort should be made to determine how much of the market's ability to predict is attributable to predicting seasonal changes in rates. The results obtained using one- and two-year maturities indicate that the market can do more than predict seasonal changes in rates.[3]

The explanation of liquidity preference presented here is based on the postulate that the risk of capital loss associated with holding short-term securities is smaller than it is for long-term securities. This implies that in a period free of trends in interest rates, price variance ought to increase with term to maturity. (It should be noted that this implication is not arithmetic. The variance in prices of three-month bills could, in principle, be greater than that of six-month bills.) If variance increases with term to maturity, then mean yields should also increase. Direct evidence of a relationship between means, price variances, and terms to maturity should be sought.

Yield curves published in the *Treasury Bulletin* constitute data that can be used to determine whether or not these propositions about variance in yields, at least to the nine-to-twelve-month range, are correct. These same data can also be used to determine what maturity constitutes the line of demarcation between increasing and decreasing variances as term to maturity increases. Finally, these data could reveal how this boundary line changes from cycle to cycle and whether these changes are correlated with differences in interest rate levels.

Although these results support the view that securities of different

---

[3] Insofar as the market can predict, one should be able to observe that underwriters' spreads increase during expansions, reach a peak at the business cycle peak, and decrease during contractions.

maturities are not perfect substitutes for one another at identical, pecuniary, holding period yields, they do not support the view that it is the time span between maturities that explains less than infinite cross elasticities. Both liquidity preference and expectations imply that the cross elasticity of demand between fifteen- and twenty-year maturities will exceed the corresponding cross elasticity for five- and ten-year maturities. In addition, the expectations hypothesis implies, for coupon bearing securities with fixed maturities, the higher the absolute level of rates, the earlier the maturity at which yield curves will flatten out. This later implication has not been tested.

Durand's findings show that negatively sloped yield curves occurred more frequently before the decade of the 1930's than they have since. This leads to the questions, do his yield curves correctly depict what, in fact, was true, and if so, why this change? Furthermore, it appears that before 1914, long-term yields frequently lagged behind cyclical turns in short-term rates, a result that does not seem consistent with either the recent behavior of these rates or with the implications of the expectations-liquidity preference hypothesis. These questions deserve a fuller investigation than this study has attempted.

DIRECTOR'S COMMENT
Paul A. Samuelson

DR. KESSEL has made a valuable contribution both on the factual and conceptual side. To a first approximation one can consider the dichotomy between (1) the *expectations* hypothesis, which supposes that people will act to make present prices approximate closely to the arithmetic mean of future prices, independently of the dispersion and higher statistical moments of the possible outcomes; and (2) the *liquidity-preference* hypothesis, which supposes that people act as if they disliked dispersion and uncertainty and will sacrifice something of first-moment of money outcome if they can thereby help hedge uncertainties. From the 1920's through 1936, the name of Keynes could be correctly associated with the second view both in the realm of commodities and securities. But to a second approximation, as a close reading of the literature will show, liquidity-preference analysis becomes more general and admits of a wider variety of empirical patterns. Thus, *before* the period of harvest when the desire to play safe is dominated by the need of producers for *long* hedges, the same Keynes-Hicks-Houthakker-Cootner analysis that leads to "normal backwardation" leads instead to its reverse: during those months, a futures price tends to fall in order to coax out risk-taking on the part of speculators. Similarly, as Modigliani, Wehrle, and others have argued, if insurance companies or other blocs of investors have a strong desire or need to "play safe" in terms of, say, eight-year periods ahead, then the yield curve might be expected to depart from its rising pattern and show a characteristic hump. Or, again, if investors in an age of secular inflation want to play safe in terms of real purchasing power, is it really anomalous that stock dividend yields should begin to fall significantly below the yield of allegedly safer fixed-principal bonds? Hence, a priori reasoning cannot itself settle what are the most plausible patterns to look for; and except as a simplifying approximation, mere dichotomy between expectation and liquidity-preference hypotheses would seem overly simple. These remarks, I should add, are of course completely within the spirit of Dr. Kessel's analysis.

APPENDIX A

THREE TESTS of the expectations hypothesis are presented in Hickman's paper. One consists of a comparison of projections of the preceding year's structure of interest rates with theoretical forecasts based on the expectations hypothesis. These results are reproduced in Table A-1.

A second test consists of a comparison between the signs of predicted and actual changes of one-year spot rates. The results of this investigation are contained in Table A-2.

Hickman found ten cases of definite disagreement with the theory. He implies that he found sixteen cases of definite agreement. On balance, this evidence does more to support than deny the validity of the Meiselman version of the expectations hypothesis.

Hickman's third test follows from the assumption that the market can forecast accurately. Hence, changes from year to year in the long-term rate should only reflect the effects of dropping last year's one-year spot rate and adding the estimate of the market for the one-year forward rate which, for the maturity observed, is the rate expected on one-year money fifty-nine years in the future.

Hickman makes the completely *ad hoc* assumption that, at most, such changes in the inputs that determine the long-term rate, according to the expectations hypothesis, will change that rate by a maximum of one basis point. How one basis point was obtained is not explained to the reader. There are no calculations showing the effect of dropping the one-year spot rate of the previous year and adding the expected one-year rate fifty-nine years into the future upon the sixty-year rate of interest. Using plus or minus five basis points as the range that defines no change in the long-term rate (this is what Durand regarded as his measurement error), Hickman found only eighteen of the forty-two years consistent with the assumption that the expectations hypothesis could predict.

Hickman does not observe that the long-term rate, for coupon bonds, is a weighted average of expected short-term rates. These weights decline monotonically as a function of time, with the current short-term rate assigned the highest weight. For a sixty-year bond with a 5 per cent coupon that yields 5 per cent to maturity, the one-year rate relevant for the sixtieth year has about one-twentieth the weight of the current one-year rate. Hence, if the one-year rate that is dropped from the average is relatively high or low compared with the other rates, yields to maturity could easily change by more than five basis points. Such a change would be completely consistent with perfect foresight.

TABLE A-1

COMPARISON OF ACTUAL AND FORECAST TERM STRUCTURES
OF INTEREST RATES, MEASURED BY AREAS UNDER CURVES[a]

Year	Type of Curve		Area Under Curve	Difference in Area Between Actual and Forecast Curves
1935	Actual		56.47	
1936	Actual		48.45	
	Projection of 1935		56.47	8.02
	Theoretical forecast from:	1935	62.92	14.47
1937	Actual		45.14	
	Projection of 1936		48.45	3.31
	Theoretical forecast from:	1936	55.00	9.86
		1935	67.30	22.16
1938	Actual		48.42	
	Projection of 1937		45.14	-3.28
	Theoretical forecast from:	1937	50.85	2.43
		1936	60.20	11.78
		1935	70.00	21.58
1939	Actual		41.29	
	Projection of 1938		48.42	7.13
	Theoretical forecast from:	1938	54.08	12.79
		1937	55.39	14.10
		1936	64.07	22.78
		1935	71.97	30.68
1940	Actual		37.42	
	Projection of 1939		41.29	3.87
	Theoretical forecast from:	1939	46.73	9.31
		1938	58.19	20.77
		1937	59.01	21.59
		1936	66.74	29.32
		1935	73.20	35.78
1941	Actual		36.25	
	Projection of 1940		37.42	1.17
	Theoretical forecast from:	1940	42.76	6.51
		1939	51.02	14.77
		1938	61.10	24.85
		1937	61.83	25.58
		1936	68.21	31.96
		1935	74.01	37.76
1942	Actual		41.28	
	Projection of 1941		36.25	-5.03
	Theoretical forecast from:	1941	41.38	.10
		1940	47.13	5.85
		1939	54.31	13.03
		1938	62.98	21.70
		1937	64.13	22.85
		1936	68.88	27.60
		1935	74.28	33.00

TABLE A-2

TYPES OF TERM STRUCTURES, THIRTY-SEVEN SELECTED YEARS (1900-42),
AND ACTUAL CHANGES IN ONE-YEAR RATES

Type of Term Structure at Beginning of Year	Number of Years in Which Prevailing	Number of Years in Which Change in Short-Term Rate to Next Year Was		
		Plus	Minus	Zero
Increasing	12	7	4[a]	1[b]
Horizontal	10	6[b]	4[b]	
Decreasing	15	6[a]	9	
Total	37	19	17	1

Source: Hickman, "Term Structure of Interest Rates," Table I,
p. III-5.

[a]Definite disagreement of historical pattern with theory.

[b]Partial disagreement of historical pattern with theory.

NOTES TO TABLE A-1

[a]The curves represent three types of structure: the actual structure of interest rates; the structure of rates in the preceding year
projected forward one year without change; and theoretical forecasts
of structures implied by structures of earlier years. The areas
under the curves are computed for the portion covering maturities of
from one to twenty-one years. For 1937, for example, the first area
in the third column is that under the curve representing the actual
term structure in 1937. The second is that under the projected curve
(the actual curve in 1936). The third and fourth areas are those
under the curves representing theoretical forecasts of the 1937 structure implied by the actual structures in 1936 and 1935, respectively.
The term structures of interest rates are represented by curves showing
the relationship between interest rates and term to maturity.

Appendix B

YIELDS TO MATURITY OF
U.S. GOVERNMENT SECURITIES,
BASED ON TREASURY YIELD CURVES

The yields shown in these tables were read from the fixed maturity yield curves published monthly in the *Treasury Bulletin*. The yields in Tables B-1 and B-2 were compiled independently by two different observers. Hence, many of the corresponding figures in the two tables differ by a few basis points. The implied forward rates shown in Tables B-1 and B-3 also differ, for the same reason.

SPOT AND FORWARD ONE-YEAR RATES

Date of Treasury Bulletin	Date of Yield Curve	One-Year Rate	Two-Year Rate	Forward One-Year Rate, One Year Hence	One-Year Rate, Observed One Year Later	Difference Between Spot and Forward One-Year Rates	Observed Change in One-Year Rate
3/58	1/58	2.20	2.50	2.83	3.53	+0.63	+1.33
4/58	2/58	1.74	2.09	2.48	3.41	+0.74	+1.67
5/58	3/58	1.75	2.09	2.47	3.53	+0.72	+1.78
6/58	4/58	1.48	1.80	2.16	3.82	+0.68	+2.34
7/58	5/58	1.14	1.66	2.31	3.88	+1.17	+2.74
8/58	6/58	1.41	1.87	2.42	4.08	+1.01	+2.67
9/58	7/58	1.65	2.07	2.56	4.30	+0.91	+2.65
10/58	8/58	2.94	3.42	3.96	4.67	+1.02	+1.73
11/58	9/58	3.35	3.53	3.72	4.89	+0.37	+1.54
12/58	10/58	3.07	3.36	3.67	4.48	+0.60	+1.41
1/59	11/58	3.27	3.48	3.70	4.93	+0.43	+1.66
2/59	12/58	3.17	3.52	3.90	4.97	+0.73	+1.80
3/59	1/59	3.53	3.80	4.09	4.62	+0.56	+1.09
4/59	2/59	3.41	3.69	3.99	4.53	+0.58	+1.12
5/59	3/59	3.53	3.87	4.24	3.73	+0.71	+0.20
6/59	4/59	3.82	4.02	4.23	4.05	+0.41	+0.23
7/59	5/59	3.88	4.21	4.56	4.04	+0.68	+0.16
8/59	6/59	4.08	4.43	4.80	3.27	+0.72	-0.81
9/59	7/59	4.30	4.53	4.77	2.89	+0.47	-1.41
10/59	8/59	4.67	4.87	5.08	2.97	+0.41	-1.70
11/59	9/59	4.89	4.95	5.01	2.93	+0.12	-1.96
12/59	10/59	4.48	4.63	4.78	2.82	+0.30	-1.66
1/60	11/59	4.93	4.97	5.01	3.03	+0.08	-1.90
2/60	12/59	4.97	5.04	5.11	2.65	+0.14	-2.32
3/60	1/60	4.62	4.76	4.90	2.78	+0.28	-1.84
4/60	2/60	4.53	4.68	4.83	3.01	+0.30	-1.52
5/60	3/60	3.73	3.89	4.06	2.91	+0.33	-0.82
6/60	4/60	4.05	4.28	4.52	2.87	+0.47	-1.18
7/60	5/60	4.04	4.26	4.49	2.91	+0.45	-1.13
8/60	6/60	3.27	3.71	4.20	3.04	+0.93	-0.23

(continued)

TABLE B-2

YIELDS OF FIXED-MATURITY TREASURY SECURITIES

Date of Treasury Bulletin	Date of Yield Curve	One-Year Rate	Two-Year Rate	Three-Year Rate	Four-Year Rate	Five-Year Rate	Six-Year Rate	Seven-Year Rate	Eight-Year Rate	Nine-Year Rate	Ten-Year Rate
3/54	1/54	1.23	1.50	1.75	1.97	2.10	2.22	2.34			
4/54	2/54	0.93	1.30	1.50	1.69	1.88	2.04	2.20			
5/54	3/54	1.00	1.30	1.50	1.68	1.84	1.99	2.13			
6/54	4/54	0.80	1.19	1.42	1.62	1.77	1.89	2.02			
7/54	5/54	0.86	1.29	1.56	1.79	1.98	2.11	2.22			
8/54	6/54	0.76	1.21	1.47	1.66	1.81	1.98	2.10			
9/54	7/54	0.70	1.16	1.46	1.67	1.85	2.01	2.11			
10/54	8/54	0.94	1.28	1.50	1.70	1.88	2.04	2.18			
11/54	9/54	1.13	1.47	1.67	1.82	1.97	2.09	2.21			
12/54	10/54	1.23	1.56	1.74	1.89	2.02	2.14	2.28			
1/55	11/54	1.22	1.54	1.75	1.94	2.09	2.22	2.35	2.44		
2/55	12/54	1.22	1.58	1.81	2.01	2.16	2.28	2.38	2.43		
3/55	1/55	1.45	1.81	2.02	2.18	2.29	2.39	2.46	2.52		
4/55	2/55	1.70	2.09	2.29	2.39	2.47	2.53	2.60	2.64		
5/55	3/55	1.67	2.04	2.27	2.39	2.48	2.55	2.60	2.64		
6/55	4/55	1.79	2.10	2.32	2.44	2.54	2.60	2.65	2.69		
7/55	5/55	1.82	2.16	2.34	2.44	2.51	2.59	2.63	2.69		
8/55	6/55	1.92	2.23	2.43	2.54	2.62	2.70	2.77	2.82		
9/55	7/55	2.13	2.43	2.61	2.72	2.82	2.88	2.91	2.92		
10/55	8/55	2.39	2.60	2.74	2.83	2.89	2.91	2.94	2.96		
11/55	9/55	2.30	2.47	2.60	2.69	2.76	2.82	2.85			
12/55	10/55	2.35	2.49	2.59	2.65	2.70	2.73	2.77			
1/56	11/55	2.61	2.74	2.81	2.83	2.84	2.86	2.88			
2/56	12/55	2.70	2.79	2.83	2.85	2.88	2.90	2.92			
3/56	1/56	2.45	2.57	2.64	2.70	2.73	2.77	2.81			
4/56	2/56	2.50	2.62	2.70	2.75	2.78	2.81	2.82			
5/56	3/56	2.59	2.88	2.97	3.00	3.02	3.03	3.05			

(continued)

TABLE B–1 (concluded)

Date of Treasury Bulletin	Date of Yield Curve	One-Year Rate	Two-Year Rate	Forward One-Year Rate, One Year Hence	One-Year Rate, Observed One Year Later	Difference between Spot and Forward One-Year Rates	Observed Change in One-Year Rate
9/60	7/60	2.89	3.11	3.34	2.96	+0.45	+0.07
10/60	8/60	2.97	3.21	3.46	3.04	+0.49	+0.07
11/60	9/60	2.93	3.21	3.51	2.99	+0.58	+0.06
12/60	10/60	2.82	3.18	3.57	2.93	+0.75	+0.11
1/61	11/60	3.03	3.33	3.65	2.99	+0.62	−0.04
2/61	12/60	2.65	2.81	2.98	3.19	+0.33	+0.54
3/61	1/61	2.78	3.15	3.56	3.22	+0.78	+0.44
4/61	2/61	3.01	3.24	3.48	3.14	+0.47	+0.13
5/61	3/61	2.91	3.16	3.43	3.00	+0.52	+0.09
6/61	4/61	2.87	3.10	3.34	3.03	+0.47	+0.16
7/61	5/61	2.91	3.24	3.60	2.99	+0.69	+0.08
8/61	6/61	3.04	3.36	3.71	3.22	+0.67	+0.18
9/61	7/61	2.96	3.33	3.73	3.36	+0.77	+0.40
10/61	8/61	3.04	3.38	3.75	3.13	+0.71	+0.09
11/61	9/61	2.99	3.37	3.79	3.01	+0.80	+0.02
12/61	10/61	2.93	3.32	3.75	2.98	+0.82	+0.05
1/62	11/61	2.99	3.36	3.76	3.09	+0.77	+0.10
1/62	12/61	3.19	3.50	3.83	3.13	+0.64	−0.06
2/62	1/62	3.22	3.58				
3/62	2/62	3.14	3.37				
4/62	3/62	3.00	3.22				
5/62	4/62	3.03	3.30				
6/62	5/62	2.99	3.20				
7/62	6/62	3.22	3.40				
8/62	7/62	3.36	3.49				
9/62	8/62	3.13	3.26				
10/62	9/62	3.01	3.19				
11/62	10/62	2.98	3.18				
12/62	11/62	3.09	3.25				
1/63	12/62	3.13	3.28				

TABLE B-2 (continued)

Date of Treasury Bulletin	Date of Yield Curve	One-Year Rate	Two-Year Rate	Three-Year Rate	Four-Year Rate	Five-Year Rate	Six-Year Rate	Seven-Year Rate	Eight-Year Rate	Nine-Year Rate	Ten-Year Rate
6/56	4/56	3.01	3.18	3.18	3.17	3.16	3.15	3.13			
7/56	5/56	2.78	2.94	2.94	2.94	2.94	2.94	2.94			
8/56	6/56	2.62	2.83	2.90	2.93	2.94	2.96				
9/56	7/56	2.84	3.15	3.21	3.22	3.23	3.23	3.23			
10/56	8/56	3.21	3.45	3.50	3.49	3.48	3.47	3.45			
11/56	9/56	3.32	3.45	3.43	3.40	3.39	3.36	3.34			
12/56	10/56	3.21	3.40	3.46	3.49	3.49	3.49				
1/57	11/56	3.57	3.74	3.69	3.65	3.63	3.60				
2/57	12/56	3.61	3.71	3.70	3.67	3.64	3.62				
3/57	1/57	3.27	3.38	3.38	3.34	3.33	3.30				
4/57	2/57	3.44	3.49	3.47	3.44	3.41	3.38				
5/57	3/57	3.37	3.47	3.48	3.47	3.44	3.41				
6/57	4/57	3.48	3.57	3.58	3.57	3.55	3.53				
7/57	5/57	3.60	3.68	3.72	3.73	3.73	3.72				
8/57	6/57	3.74	3.88	3.90	3.97	3.97	3.96				
9/57	7/57	3.82	3.93	3.98	4.01	4.02	4.01				
10/57	8/57	4.02	4.02	3.97	3.94	3.90	3.86				
11/57	9/57	4.09	4.09	4.07	4.06	4.04	4.03	4.02	4.02	4.01	4.01
12/57	10/57	3.98	4.05	4.06	4.06	4.05	4.03	4.01	3.99	3.98	3.97
1/58	11/57	3.44	3.43	3.40	3.38	3.37	3.35	3.35	3.36	3.40	3.43
2/58	12/57	2.88	2.87	2.85	2.84	2.84	2.87	2.92	2.96	3.01	3.04
3/58	1/58	2.19	2.48	2.68	2.78	2.84	2.92	2.98	3.06	3.12	3.17
4/58	2/58	1.73	2.07	2.31	2.50	2.64	2.75	2.85	2.94	3.00	3.05
5/58	3/58	1.71	2.09	2.33	2.48	2.59	2.70	2.78	2.86	2.92	2.98
6/58	4/58	1.46	1.78	2.07	2.26	2.42	2.57	2.69	2.78	2.86	2.91
7/58	5/58	1.09	1.60	1.98	2.18	2.36	2.50	2.60	2.71	2.79	2.88
8/58	6/58	1.47	1.90	2.25	2.48	2.60	2.71	2.81	2.88	2.95	3.20

(continued)

TABLE B-2 (continued)

Date of Treasury Bulletin	Date of Yield Curve	One-Year Rate	Two-Year Rate	Three-Year Rate	Four-Year Rate	Five-Year Rate	Six-Year Rate	Seven-Year Rate	Eight-Year Rate	Nine-Year Rate	Ten-Year Rate
9/58	7/58	1.68	2.09	2.45	2.70	2.86	2.96	3.05	3.11	3.18	3.21
10/58	8/58	3.01	3.42	3.54	3.59	3.63	3.67	3.70	3.74	3.75	3.77
11/58	9/58	3.38	3.53	3.62	3.70	3.74	3.76	3.78	3.79	3.81	3.82
12/58	10/58	3.09	3.35	3.55	3.70	3.76	3.80	3.81	3.82	3.82	3.82
1/59	11/58	3.29	3.48	3.68	3.64	3.66	3.67	3.68	3.69	3.70	3.71
2/59	12/58	3.20	3.53	3.70	3.80	3.85	3.85	3.85	3.84	3.84	3.84
3/59	1/59	3.52	3.80	3.91	3.97	3.98	3.98	3.98	3.97	3.97	3.96
4/59	2/59	3.42	3.70	3.79	3.83	3.85	3.87	3.88	3.89	3.90	3.90
5/59	3/59	3.52	3.86	3.96	4.02	4.02	4.02	4.02	4.02	4.02	4.02
6/59	4/59	3.81	4.02	4.12	4.18	4.23	4.23	4.23	4.22	4.21	4.20
7/59	5/59	3.92	4.20	4.29	4.28	4.27	4.25	4.25	4.23	4.21	4.20
8/59	6/59	4.08	4.45	4.49	4.47	4.45	4.42	4.38	4.34	4.32	4.29
9/59	7/59	4.28	4.55	4.57	4.54	4.48	4.45	4.42	4.39	4.36	4.33
10/59	8/59	4.67	4.88	4.90	4.84	4.74	4.67	4.60	4.55	4.50	4.47
11/59	9/59	4.90	4.95	4.92	4.84	4.77	4.73	4.68	4.64	4.60	4.57
12/59	10/59	4.47	4.64	4.70	4.67	4.60	4.55	4.49	4.45	4.41	4.37
1/60	11/59	4.94	4.97	4.93	4.84	4.76	4.69	4.62	4.57	4.51	4.47
2/60	12/59	4.97	5.04	5.06	5.05	5.01	4.96	4.90	4.84	4.79	4.73
3/60	1/60	4.60	4.75	4.80	4.79	4.75	4.70	4.66	4.62	4.57	4.55
4/60	2/60	4.52	4.68	4.74	4.74	4.67	4.61	4.55	4.49	4.46	4.44
5/60	3/60	3.67	3.89	3.97	4.03	4.08	4.10	4.10	4.10	4.10	4.10
6/60	4/60	4.04	4.29	4.37	4.40	4.39	4.36	4.33	4.31	4.29	4.28
7/60	5/60	3.98	4.25	4.33	4.37	4.36	4.31	4.28	4.25	4.22	4.20
8/60	6/60	3.21	3.70	3.89	3.97	4.00	4.02	4.02	4.02	4.02	4.02
9/60	7/60	2.86	3.12	3.29	3.41	3.52	3.60	3.66	3.70	3.73	3.77
10/60	8/60	2.93	3.19	3.37	3.50	3.61	3.68	3.72	3.76	3.79	3.80
11/60	9/60	2.92	3.22	3.39	3.54	3.63	3.69	3.71	3.75	3.78	3.80
12/60	10/60	2.86	3.21	3.42	3.58	3.69	3.76	3.80	3.82	3.86	3.88

(continued)

TABLE B-2 (concluded)

Date of Treasury Bulletin	Date of Yield Curve	One-Year Rate	Two-Year Rate	Three-Year Rate	Four-Year Rate	Five-Year Rate	Six-Year Rate	Seven-Year Rate	Eight-Year Rate	Nine-Year Rate	Ten-Year Rate
1/61	11/60	3.02	3.37	3.58	3.70	3.79	3.87	3.90	3.95	3.98	3.99
2/61	12/60	2.65	2.93	3.18	3.35	3.48	3.57	3.61	3.65	3.68	3.70
3/61	1/61	2.78	3.13	3.46	3.61	3.68	3.72	3.75	3.73	3.80	3.82
4/61	2/61	2.99	3.23	3.40	3.52	3.58	3.61	3.63	3.66	3.69	3.70
5/61	3/61	2.90	3.12	3.31	3.48	3.59	3.65	3.70	3.75	3.78	3.80
6/61	4/61	2.86	3.08	3.25	3.38	3.48	3.56	3.62	3.68	3.70	3.71
7/61	5/61	2.99	3.26	3.42	3.53	3.64	3.70	3.75	3.79	3.30	3.80
8/61	6/61	2.99	3.34	3.56	3.67	3.75	3.80	3.82	3.87	3.88	3.89
9/61	7/61	2.92	3.32	3.61	3.78	3.88	3.90	3.92	3.92	3.92	3.92
10/61	8/61	3.00	3.40	3.72	3.88	3.94	3.97	3.99	4.00	4.01	4.01
11/61	9/61	2.97	3.38	3.61	3.70	3.74	3.77	3.80	3.82	3.85	3.88
12/61	10/61	2.82	3.29	3.56	3.65	3.72	3.78	3.80	3.82	3.85	3.87
1/62	11/61	2.96	3.37	3.61	3.72	3.82	3.89	3.93	3.96	3.98	3.99
1/62	12/61	3.21	3.50	3.68	3.80	3.86	3.90	3.93	3.96	3.99	4.01
2/62	1/62	3.22	3.59	3.79	3.91	3.97	4.02	4.05	4.08	4.10	4.12
3/62	2/62	3.18	3.38	3.52	3.66	3.77	3.84	3.90	3.96	4.01	4.03
4/62	3/62	3.00	3.22	3.38	3.51	3.61	3.69	3.77	3.82	3.86	3.88
5/62	4/62	3.03	3.27	3.44	3.57	3.65	3.72	3.78	3.82	3.85	3.88
6/62	5/62	3.00	3.22	3.38	3.54	3.64	3.74	3.82	3.88	3.90	3.91
7/62	6/62	3.22	3.40	3.54	3.66	3.77	3.83	3.90	3.96	3.99	4.00
8/62	7/62	3.31	3.48	3.61	3.71	3.82	3.91	3.98	4.01	4.02	4.03
9/62	8/62	3.11	3.25	3.38	3.51	3.65	3.78	3.88	3.92	3.95	3.95
10/62	9/62	2.98	3.18	3.32	3.48	3.65	3.75	3.83	3.90	3.92	3.95
11/62	10/62	2.96	3.16	3.32	3.49	3.63	3.73	3.82	3.88	3.91	3.92
12/62	11/62	3.08	3.24	3.38	3.50	3.59	3.67	3.75	3.82	3.88	3.92

TABLE B-3

SPOT AND FORWARD ONE-YEAR RATES ADJUSTED FOR LIQUIDITY PREMIUMS

Date of Yield Curve	One-Year Rate	Forward One-Year Rate One Year Hence	Estimated Liquidity Premium	Forward Rate Minus Liquidity Premium	One-Year Rate Observed One Year Later
4/58	1.46	2.17	-0.34	2.51	3.81
5/58	1.09	2.34	-0.53	2.87	3.92
6/58	1.47	2.45	-0.34	2.79	4.08
7/58	1.68	2.60	-0.23	2.83	4.28
8/58	3.01	3.88	+0.43	3.45	4.68
9/58	3.38	3.68	+0.62	3.06	4.90
10/58	3.09	3.63	+0.74	2.89	4.47
11/58	3.29	3.68	+0.77	2.91	4.94
12/58	3.20	3.89	+0.87	3.02	4.97
1/59	3.52	4.10	+0.98	3.12	4.60
2/59	3.42	4.00	+0.93	3.07	4.52
3/59	3.52	4.23	+1.04	3.19	3.67
4/59	3.81	4.24	+1.05	3.19	4.04
5/59	3.92	4.50	+1.18	3.32	3.98
6/59	4.08	4.85	+1.35	3.50	3.21
7/59	4.28	4.83	+1.34	3.49	2.86
8/59	4.67	5.09	+1.47	3.62	2.93
9/59	4.90	5.00	+1.43	3.57	2.92
10/59	4.47	4.81	+1.33	3.48	2.86
11/59	4.94	5.00	+1.43	3.57	3.02
12/59	4.97	5.11	+1.48	3.63	2.65
1/60	4.60	4.90	+1.38	3.52	2.78
2/60	4.52	4.84	+1.35	3.49	2.99
3/60	3.67	4.12	+0.99	3.13	2.90
4/60	4.04	4.55	+1.20	3.35	2.86
5/60	3.98	4.53	+1.19	3.34	2.99
6/60	3.21	4.26	+1.06	3.20	2.99
7/60	2.86	3.40	+0.63	2.77	2.92
8/60	2.93	3.47	+0.66	2.81	3.00
9/60	2.92	3.55	+0.70	2.85	2.97
10/60	2.86	3.60	+0.73	2.87	2.82
11/60	3.02	3.76	+0.81	2.95	2.96
12/60	2.65	3.23	+0.54	2.69	3.21
1/61	2.78	3.52	+0.69	2.83	3.22
2/61	2.99	3.48	+0.67	2.81	3.18